BY HAND

25 Beautiful Objects to Make in the American Folk Art Tradition

Lady of Liberty, Alice Strom; 1999. Basswood, acrylic paint: h. 23 in. (58.4 cm) w. 19 in. (48.3 cm) d. 2½ in. (6.4 cm). Photo by artist

BY HAND

25 Beautiful Objects to Make in the American Folk Art Tradition

Janice Eaton Kilby

with the assistance of Veronika Alice Gunter

LARK BOOKS

A Division of Sterling Publishing Co., Inc.
New York

Assistant Editor: **Veronika Alice Gunter**
Art Direction and Production: **Celia Naranjo**
Photography: **Evan Bracken**
Illustrations: **Orrin Lundgren**
Editorial Assistance: **Rain Newcomb, Murphy Townsend**
Art Assistant: **Hannes Charen**

Library of Congress Cataloging-in-Publication Data
Kilby, Janice Eaton, 1955–
    By hand: 25 beautiful objects to make in the American folk art tradition / by Janice Eaton Kilby,
with the assistance of Veronika Alice Gunter.
        p. cm.
    Includes index.
    ISBN 1-57990-242-1
    [1. Handicraft—United States.] I. Title.
    TT157.K435 2001
    745.5'0973--dc21   00-054974

10 9 8 7 6 5 4 3 2 1

Published by Lark Books, a division of
Sterling Publishing Co., Inc.
387 Park Avenue South, New York, N.Y. 10016

© 2001, Lark Books

Distributed in Canada by Sterling Publishing,
c/o Canadian Manda Group, One Atlantic Ave., Suite 105
Toronto, Ontario, Canada M6K 3E7

Distributed in the U.K. by:
Guild of Master Craftsman Publications Ltd., Castle Place, 166 High Street,
Lewes, East Sussex, England, BN7 1XU
Tel: (+ 44) 1273 477374
Fax: (+ 44) 1273 478606
Email: pubs@thegmcgroup.com
Web: www.gmcpublications.com

Distributed in Australia by Capricorn Link (Australia) Pty Ltd., P.O. Box 704, Windsor, NSW 2756, Australia

If you have questions or comments about this book, please contact:
Lark Books
50 College St.
Asheville, NC 28801
(828) 253-0467

Printed in China

ISBN 1-57990-242-1

contents

Proud Canticleer, Alice Strom, 1999. Painted wood carving.
12½ x 4 inches (31.8 x 10.2 cm). Private collection.

introduction

Democratic nations will habitually prefer the useful to the beautiful, and they will require that the beautiful be useful.

Alexis de Tocqueville, *Democracy in America*, 1835-1840

I come by my interest in folk art honestly, as we Southerners say. When I was growing up in Georgia in the 1950s and '60s, I had a mother who loved old things and was a fan of folk art before the term became widely used. I lost count of the times we'd be driving somewhere in the car on a fine day in the country, and Mother

Sea Gull Decoy, William D. Sarni; 1998. White pine, acrylic paint: h. 13 in. (33 cm) w. 15 in. (38.1 cm) d. 7 in. (17.8 cm). Photo by artist

would suddenly spot a dusty old junk store or a barn sprouting with weirdly rusting tools and appliances. Out we'd get, and she'd crank up the Southern charm, chatting with the proprietor or property owner. Before you knew it, they'd be digging in tubs of dusty whatnots, or crawling out of haylofts clutching a prize that put a gleam in her eye. A little more talk (sometimes a *lot* more talk), then a little money exchanged hands, and we'd drive off with the day's booty in the car trunk, happy.

Clearly, collecting folk art inspires happiness, but what exactly is folk art, and what did it mean to the people who made it? Those questions have provoked decades of spirited argument among collectors, craftspeople, museum curators, academics, and critics. They still don't all agree on the answer, though the tent that encompasses folk art has gotten bigger lately.

Double Wedding Ring Quilt, quiltmaker unidentified, probably Georgia; 1930-1940. Cotton. Collection of the Museum of American Folk Art, New York; gift of Robert Bishop. 1993.04.19

If you ask an average American what folk art is, an honest response might be, "I know it when I see it." People recognize certain objects that have been part of America's daily life for the past several hundred years, such as treasured quilts, beautiful baskets, eagle weathervanes, or funny little whirligigs.

If an item is folk art, it's useful; it has a reason for being beyond mere beauty of decoration. Yet, an item is also folk art because its maker took the time to add a pleasingly decorative or aesthetic element beyond brute utility. Folk art blurs the distinctions between art and craft. Folk art is direct, honest, and unconcerned with what fine-art schools or theorists think art is. Folk art can also be the expression of sheer whimsy on the part of the maker. It's a means of amusing oneself, giving pleasure to others, or passing the time. Folk art can be the expression of a personal compulsion or spiritual vision, the kind of motives that won't let a person rest until he's acted; this is the special category of work

Farmhouse Bright, Lisa Curry Mair; 1998. Canvas floorcloth, acrylic paint: h. 30 in. (76.2 cm) w. 45 in. (114.3 cm). Photo by artist

called *visionary* or *outsider* art. Folk art uses what's at hand and it makes do—values that Americans still cherish.

Folk art is not created in a vacuum. Context is critical: the objects made by early Americans were directly influenced by everything

Talk Softly and Ride a Tall Chicken, Alice Strom; 1998. Basswood, acrylic paint: h. 17½ in. (44.5 cm) w. 11 in. (27.9 cm) d. 5 in. (12.7 cm). Photo by artist

Ring Box, Willis Coleman (1876-1964); c. 1912. Courtesy of the John & Linda Sholl Collection

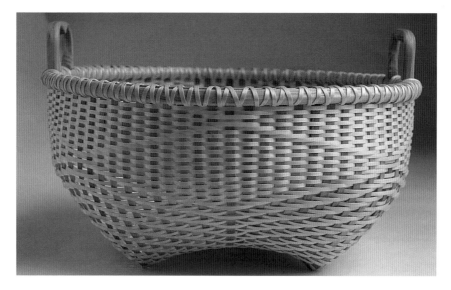

from the materials available in nearby forests to the import restrictions England enforced before we Americans held our famous tea party. Today's folk artists respond to their physical environment and cultural influences, too.

Folk art is familiar. It's an expression of who we think we are as a country, and it's democratic. In the country and the city, it continues to be made by successive generations of communities and families, and by the per-

Top left: Watch Stand (detail), Charles B. Toby; 1819, Cape Horn, Chile. Bone, baleen, wood, paper, metal. 8⁵/₁₆ x 3¹/₂ x 2¹/₃ inches (21.1 x 8.9 x 5.4 cm). From the collections of The Mariners' Museum, Newport News, Va.

Top right: Quatrefoil Cathead Basket, Debra Paulson; 1999. Black ash splint: h. 8 in. (20.3 cm) w. 9 in. (22.9 cm) d. 9 in. (22.9 cm). Photo by artist

Bottom right: American Trilogy: FREEDOM, EQUALITY, LIBERTY, Susan Feller; 1999-2000. Hand hooked with wool strips of fabric: h. 45 in. (114.3 cm) w. 54 in. (137.2 cm). Photo by Billy Prouty Photographers

son inspired to create a one-of-a-kind object rather than just buying something mass-produced.

The aim of this book is to combine a how-to craft book with an informative survey of several significant categories of American folk art. You'll learn how to make a selection of beautiful, traditional objects using many techniques and decorative effects that would have been familiar to craftspeople hundreds of years ago and are still used by professional artisans and amateurs today.

Even if you've never made a handcrafted anything before, *By Hand* will show you how to make baskets, quilts, a cross-stitched sampler, carved wood and chip art, folded paper work, memoryware, rugs, scrimshaw, silhouettes, smithed and painted tin, painted and stenciled furnishings, and rustic furniture and accessories from twigs and bark.

The projects are easy to make, but you won't be cheating in terms of the techniques you'll use (except for scrimshaw; these days we're admiring whales, not hunting them). The how-to techniques are authentic within reason (you won't have to chop down a tree in order to whittle a fish decoy). The results will be something beautiful you can use or put on display or both. Best of all, you'll have the satisfaction of knowing that you're literally connected to, and working within, a long, long heritage of American craft. If you believe in ghosts, don't worry. They'll all be friendly and smiling in approval over your shoulder while you work.

By Hand also includes surveys of the histories of a dozen categories of folk art objects, with superb photographs of significant museum pieces and work created by many of the finest traditional craftspeople in America today, the same people who were also kind enough to design projects for this book. That's part of what folk art is about. It's not dead and dusty, and it's not restricted to objects sold in galleries or auctions. It's a living, breathing body of knowledge and tradition. The tradition takes shape in the hands of its makers and is then passed on, often one-on-one. Hopefully, we've made this book in that same respectful spirit.

Quilt Patterns, Susan Feller; 1998. Hand hooked and quilted rug: h. 54 in. (137.2 cm) w. 24 in. (61 cm). Photo by Billy Prouty Photographers

painting and stenciling

*I wonder that the floor does not give way under the visitor while he is admiring the gewgaws upon the mantel-piece....
I cannot but perceive that this so-called rich and refined life is a thing jumped at, and I do not get on in the enjoyment of
the fine arts which adorn it, my attention being wholly occupied with the jump...*

Henry David Thoreau, *Walden,* 1854

Chest of Drawers, artist unknown, probably New Hampshire; c. 1800. Painted and grained pine and maple: h. 46 in. (116.8 cm) w. 37 in. (94 cm) d. 17¾ in. (45.1 cm). Collection of the Museum of American Folk Art, New York; Museum of American Folk Art purchase. 1981.12.25

Most early American furniture was of simple construction and made from locally-available woods, such as pine and poplar. Painting was the favored method for decorating the plain wood surfaces or for hiding crude construction or mismatched wood. Many of the colors would have looked garish to our modern eyes; among the pieces that survive, time has caused protective coatings of varnish or shellac to darken, dulling the original hues.

PAINTING TECHNIQUES
It was especially popular in New England to paint and decorate large pieces of furniture and smaller items such as boxes. Painted pine blanket chests with lids were common in the region, and the earliest American furniture handpainted with decorative motifs was made in the late 1600s and early 1700s in Connecticut. Painted and stencilled design motifs reflected the fact that America was an agrarian nation, and fruit, flowers, and leaves were popular. Paint was used differently in the South, where craftsmen used three or four different colors of paint to highlight the architectural elements of one piece of furniture. The center panels of a door might be one color, surrounded by a frame of a different color.

The German immigrants who settled in southeastern Pennsylvania (and were mistakenly nicknamed the Pennsylvania Dutch) are well-known for the hearts, tulips, urns, mermaids, birds, the tree of life, and other decorative motifs derived from early German folk art. Their craftsmen and itinerant decorators used stencils, grain painting, and freehand painting to adorn furniture. Young girls traditionally received an *ausschteier kischt*, or dower chest, in which they accumulated part of their dowry, for instance, the linens, clothing, and other necessities for their eventual marriage and new home. The massive, freestanding *schrank* was less common; it served as a communal wardrobe for a family to store clothing, and was often elaborately decorated with paint.

Most Pennsylvania Dutch families owned a chest with a lift top for storing clothing. Carefully crafted from pine or tulip wood, the chests were decorated with characteristic motifs. Vivid, oil-based greens, blues, reds, and oranges were used, with contrasts in black, brown, and white. Painting techniques were often mixed. Most makers of early painted furniture are unknown to us today, but styles of specific regions can be discerned. A group of chests produced in Berks County, Pennsylvania, during the late 1700s and early 1800s feature striking unicorns, seated horsemen, and birds. Most of the Pennsylvania Dutch painted furniture known to us was made before 1800, with the exception of a group of chests and desks made in the Mahantago Valley up to the mid-1830s. That furniture is distinguished by a dark green base color, tiny stenciled daisies, and painted yellow and red birds. The Germans migrated to several other states, including Texas and Virginia, where Johannes Spitler used a compass to create complex, painted geometric designs for furniture that are well-known to collectors today.

Grain painting was a technique commonly used by early Americans to decorate wood with paint. First, a base coat of light-colored paint is applied to wood and allowed to dry. A second coat of darker paint is laid on top of the first and, while it's still wet, combs or brushes are used freehand to manipulate the wet paint to imitate the grain patterns of expensive or strikingly figured woods. The Federal-style sideboard table shown in the photograph above features graining applied with a feather

Above: Federal Sideboard Table, artist unknown, New England; 1820-1835. Grain painted and decorated wood, brass knobs: h. 34⅞ in. (88.6 cm) w. 26 in. (66 cm) d. 20 in. (50.8 cm). Collection of the Museum of American Folk Art, New York; Eva and Morris Feld Folk Art Acquisition Fund. 1981.12.06

Left: Dower Chest with Mermaid Decoration, artist unknown, Pennsylvania; dated 1790. Painted and decorated pine, iron: h. 24¾ in. (62.9 cm) w. 50½ (128.3 cm) d. 23¾ in. (60.3 cm). Collection of the Museum of American Folk Art, New York; Museum of American Folk Art purchase. 1981.12.04

Above right: Marbled and Smoke Grained Rug, Janet Flinchbaugh; 1998. Floorcloth: h. 24 in. (61 cm) w. 36 in. (91.4 cm). Photo by artist. This contemporary rendition of a traditional floorcloth uses smoke decoration very effectively.

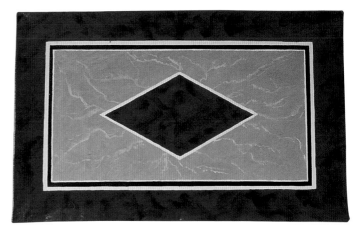

and sponge to imitate a variety of exotic woods often used for inlays in fine cabinetry. Black paint grained over red paint of a medium hue creates a good simulation of prized (and expensive) tropical rosewood, and yellow ochre paint serves as the base coat for many other wood simulations. During the process, the colored glazes set quickly, and therefore patterns had to be created quickly. Professional painters typically completed one side, or a single surface element, before going on to another.

One of the great nineteenth-century professional paint decorators in New England was Moses Eaton. The photograph below shows Eaton's actual sample box, which contained representative panels of 10 different surface treatments. Clients could pick the treatments they wanted for their furniture. Eaton's box also contained several stencil brushes and 78 stencils which made 40 complete designs. The stencils were made of heavy paper stiffened with paint and oil, and were cut with a

beveled edge to ensure the painted designs retained a sharp edge. Eaton stenciled homes in Maine, Massachusetts, and New Hampshire for hundreds of clients in the early decades of the 1800s.

Furniture decorators often let their imaginations, instead of nature, inspire the colors and painted patterns they used, as shown in the photograph on page 13 of a case clock spotted with "paw prints." The prints possibly were created with sponges or crumpled paper. Rags, corncobs, trimmed brushes, pieces of putty or leather, fingertips, and the prints of the sides, heels, and palms of hands were also used by furniture decorators to great effect. If linseed oil and vinegar or another solvent was added to the second coat of paint, which was then textured with rags, the paint dried unevenly, flowing and bleeding into swirling patterns.

In the first half of the 1800s, smoke was also used to decorate wood, a technique also used in the contemporary floorcloth shown above. A light-colored base coat was painted on and allowed to dry. Varnish was then applied and, before it dried, a lit candle was passed near the wet surface, leaving decorative soot marks. Stencils and cutouts placed on the surface were also used to create patterns and figures with the soot.

Below: Sample Box and Ten Panels, Moses Eaton Jr. (1796-1886), Dublin, New Hampshire; c. 1800-1830. Painted and decorated pine, brass. Collection of the Museum of American Folk Art, New York; anonymous gift and gift of the Richard Coyle Lilly Foundation. 1980.28.1A-K

STENCILING TECHNIQUES

Stenciling was another very popular method of decorating wooden furniture, as well as floors and walls. Starting in the early nineteenth century, decorators imitated elaborate gilded Empire-style chairs, painting them by hand, sometimes with gold leaf or powder. Less-skilled craftsmen used stencils and less-expensive metallic powders to achieve the same effect. Precut cardboard or metal stencils were laid on a wooden surface which had been primed with varnish and allowed to almost dry. A velvet pad was used to brush metallic powder into perforations in the stencil to create a precisely-patterned design, which was then sealed with varnish. Some early stencil designs were very complicated; one piece of fruit might use seven separate stencils.

As stenciled decorations became more affordable to more people, they reached the height of their popularity between 1820 and 1840. Amateurs used stenciling, too, and during the first half of the nineteenth century, young women in finishing schools learned to paint wood freehand and to use stencils.

In the 1820s, manufacturer Lambert Hitchcock (1785-1852) introduced mass-produced, stenciled chairs in a well-known design from his Connecticut factory, and other, smaller workshops in several states manufactured their own stenciled chairs. Although he may not have invented the design, Hitchcock clearly popularized it so that it is now forever known as the Hitchcock chair. The painted wooden side chair had a rush seat, and it was decorated with floral stencils on its central back slat, plus gilding and striping applied freehand by artisans. As the demand for stenciled furniture grew, however, manufacturers inevitably took shortcuts, reducing the number of stencils used, simplifying the designs, and taking less care to apply the powders subtly.

Unfortunately, hand-crafted furniture could not compete in terms of cost with factory-made pieces, and by the mid-1800s, mass production had largely replaced individual craftsmanship.

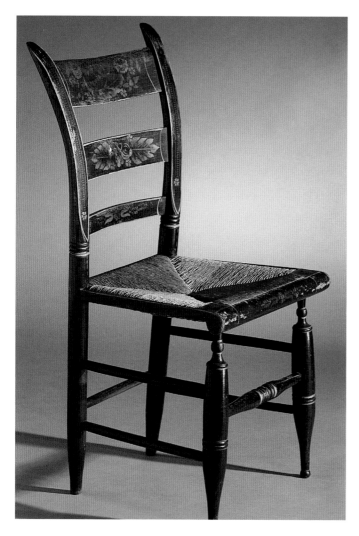

Hitchcock Chair, Lambert Hitchcock; circa 1815-1820. h. 34¼ inches (87 cm), d. 15 inches (38.1 cm), w. 17⅓ inches (44 cm). © Shelburne Museum, Shelburne, Vermont.

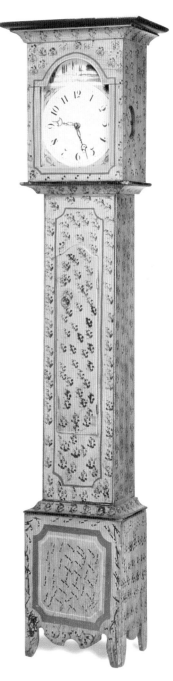

Tall Case Clock, case: artist unknown, clockworks: Lambert W. Lewis, Trumbull County, Ohio; 1812-1834. Painted and decorated pine case, wooden works: h. 87 in. (221 cm) w. 21½ in. (54.6 cm) d. 12¾ in. (32.4 cm). Collection of the Museum of American Folk Art, New York; Eva and Morris Feld Folk Art Acquistion Fund. 1981.12.22

painted wood grain chair

EARLY SETTLERS FREQUENTLY PAINTED SIMPLE WOOD FURNISHINGS WITH GRAINS THAT SIMULATED MORE EXPENSIVE WOODS. THEIR IMAGINATIONS ALSO RAN RIOT WITH COLORS AND DECORATIVE EFFECTS NEVER SEEN IN NATURE! BELIEVE IT OR NOT, YOU'LL USE EVERYDAY ITEMS SUCH AS COTTON SWABS AND A CORK TO CREATE THESE MAGNIFICENT TEXTURES. THIS PROJECT ALSO TEACHES YOU USEFUL TECHNIQUES FOR SIMULATING BURLED AND HEARTWOOD GRAINS. FEEL FREE TO ADAPT THE INSTRUCTIONS TO FIT THE CHAIR OF YOUR CHOICE.

DIANE N. KILLEEN,
Designer

Materials

– Wood chair
– Oil primer (optional)
– Tack cloth
– Spray paint in red or another bright color of your choice
– Small tubes of artist's oil paint in black, raw umber, burnt umber, olive green, and violet*
– Translucent oil glazing liquid*
– Red mahogany wood stain (optional)
– Metallic gold oil paint (optional)
  *Available in artist's supply stores

Tools and Supplies

– Paintbrush
– Small mixing bowls
– Spoon or wooden craft stick
– Bristle brush, ½ inch (1.3 cm) wide
– Cosmetic foam wedges
– Badger brush
– Turpentine or mineral spirits
– Cork from a wine bottle, or cork of similar size
– Cotton swabs
– Small artist's brush
– Rag

Instructions

1. If the chair is already painted, you'll need to paint the surface with the oil primer. Apply it with the paintbrush and let dry.

2. Wipe the chair with the tack cloth to remove any dirt and lint, then spray the red paint over the entire surface. Let dry.

3. You'll mix three different glazes to paint the "grain" on the chair. To make glaze number one, combine approximately 3 tablespoons (45 mL) of translucent oil glazing liquid with ½ to 1 teaspoon (2.5 to 5 mL) each of the burnt umber and black artist's oil paints in a small mixing bowl, using the spoon or craft stick to mix them well. Use the same quantities of glaze and paint in the glazes you make below; the object is to create a deep, rich-colored glaze that you can still see through.

4. Use the ½-inch (1.3 cm) brush to paint the glaze on all the small bars of the chair, completing one bar before starting the next. When you've covered an entire bar, use the tip of a cosmetic foam wedge to wipe away the glaze in short, jerky motions, making marks that resemble tiger stripes (see photo 1). Be sure to wipe around the entire bar, including its underside and back side. Badger the surfaces of the bars by lightly brushing them with the soft badger brush.

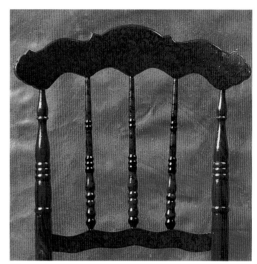
Photo 1

5. Mix glaze number two in a small bowl by combining the translucent glazing liquid and the raw umber and olive green paint. Mix well.

6. After thoroughly cleaning the ½-inch (1.3 cm) brush with turpentine, use the brush to paint the entire seat with the second glaze. Pressing the flat end of the cork against the newly painted surface, swirl the glaze in a circular motion all over the seat, overlapping the swirls to simulate a knotted burl wood grain (see photo 2). Repeat the painting and swirling processes on the other flat areas of the seat. For added interest, dab on tiny spots of green paint and

Photo 2

swirl them into the pattern you've already formed. Because you're using oil-based paints and glaze, you can add these effects without interrupting the overall pattern.

7. Mix glaze number three by combining the translucent glazing liquid and the violet and black. Mix well.

8. Clean the ½-inch (1.3 cm) brush with turpentine. You'll use the brush to paint all four of the leg uprights with the third glaze, but you'll work one leg at a time, painting it and completing its textural effects before proceeding to the next leg. After you cover a leg with glaze, use a cotton swab to wipe it away in a vertical stripe pattern that starts at the top of the leg and ends in the foot (see photo 3). The lines should run parallel with each other but don't have to be straight; slightly curved lines are more interesting and their inconsistency better simulates wood grain. You can also simulate heartgrain by wiping away the

Photo 3

glaze in an elongated arch motion, starting small and narrow and following with additional lines, as you would when drawing a rainbow. As the arches get higher, they elongate and eventually join up with the vertical stripes. Badger the leg with the dry badger brush, slightly blending the bands. Repeat step 8 on each remaining leg. Let dry.

9. Use the small artist's brush and black paint to paint any turnings in the chair bars and legs as desired (see photo 4). Let dry.

Photo 4

10. To unify the areas decorated with the burl wood texture, use the ½-inch (1.3 cm) brush to paint on the mahogany wood stain, then wipe with the rag, leaving a thin film of stain. Let dry.

11. If your chair has a woven seat, decorate it if desired by using the small artist's brush (after cleaning with turpentine) to add small spots of the metallic gold paint at intersections of the weaving, as shown in photo 5. Let dry.

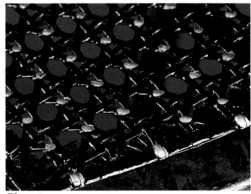

Photo 5

Fantasy Wood Grain Box

Would you believe a cut potato, an eraser, and an old business card are among the simple tools used to create the gorgeous surface effects on this wooden box? When you make this piece, you'll be carrying on the tradition of faux surface graining and patterning practiced by early American furniture painters. Before decorating your box, you may want to practice creating different textures on a painted scrap of wood.

Diane N. Killeen,
Designer

MATERIALS

- Wooden box* (the one in the photograph measures 9¼ x 18 x 9½ inches [23.5 x 45.7 x 24.1 cm])
- Latex wood primer
- Latex semigloss paint in bright orange or yellow
- Translucent glaze in greenish-blue, yellow ocher, and maize**
- Acrylic craft paint in Van Dyke red
- Mahogany wood stain

TOOLS AND SUPPLIES

- Wood putty (optional)
- Sandpaper, 220 grit or finer
- Rag
- Screwdriver
- Soft pencil
- Painter's tape
- 3 bristle or foam brushes, ½ inch (8.9 cm) wide
- Potato, cut into a square shape
- Badger brush or any soft, dry brush***
- Square eraser
- Small mixing box
- Old business card, or piece of cardboard the same size

*Boxes are available at craft stores, or you can find them at flea markets.

**Glazes are sold at hardware stores and home improvement centers. You can also tint clear acrylic glaze with green, red, black, and orange acrylic paints to achieve the desired colors.

***Available at craft and art supply stores

INSTRUCTIONS

1. If the box has holes or imperfections you don't find pleasing, fill them with the wood putty and let dry. Sand, then wipe off the dust with a dampened rag.

2. Use the screwdriver to remove any handles, hinges, or other hardware you don't wish to paint.

3. Sand the box until the surface is smooth to the touch. Wipe clean, then paint it with the latex primer. Let dry, then paint with the orange or yellow latex paint. Let dry again.

4. Referring to figures 1, 2, and 3, use the pencil to very lightly sketch the various borders and accents directly onto the box.

5. Refer to figure 1. Use the painter's masking tape to tape off the areas where you'll apply glaze number one (greenish-blue) to the front and back of the box and the lid. Use the ½-inch (1.3 cm) paintbrush to brush on the glaze in small areas to prevent premature drying. Immediately apply the edge of the potato square in small, parallel jerks to lift and dab the glaze from the surface, creating horizontal marks (see photo 1). Next, badger the surface by lightly brushing over it with the soft, dry brush to soften the pattern's edges. Let dry.

6. Refer to figure 2. Tape off the areas on the top of the lid and the box sides to be painted with glaze number two, the yellow ochre.

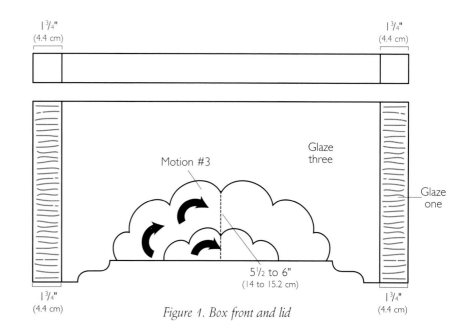

Figure 1. Box front and lid

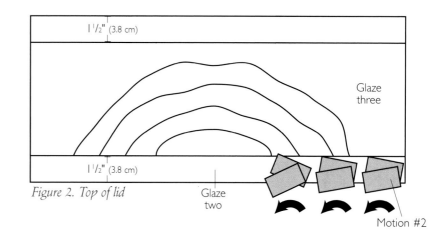

Figure 2. Top of lid

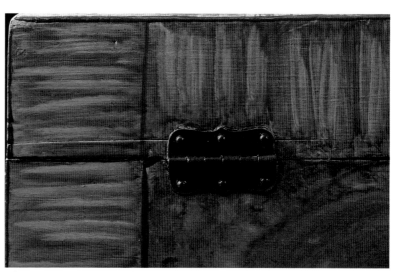

Photo 1

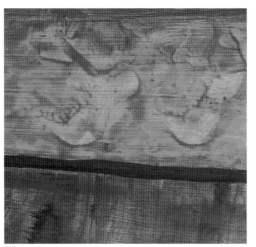

Photo 2

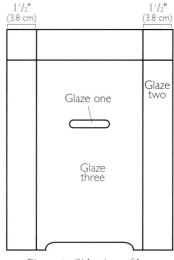

Figure 3. Side view of box

Apply the glaze in small areas, then place the flat part of the eraser against the box at an angle and twist the eraser into an upright position (see photo 2). Badger the surface with the soft, dry brush. Let dry.

7. Prepare glaze number three by mixing a small amount of the Van Dyke red acrylic paint with the maize glaze in the bowl. Refer to figures 1 and 2. Tape off the areas to be painted with glaze 3. Apply the glaze with a brush, then drag the long edge of the business card through the glaze, making a flower shape. Work from the bottom up and around, dragging different sides of the card in a swirl to form different-sized bands resembling grained wood from the heart of a tree (see photo 3). In the areas outside the

bands, use your fingertips to create dots and other textures that please you. Badger with the dry brush and let dry.

8. Refer to figure 3. Use the tape to mask the areas you already painted with glaze number one on the sides of the box. Apply glaze number 3 where indicated. Hold the business card perpendicular to the surface. Gripping one end of the card with your fingers, drag the other end through the glaze in short, jerky motions, lifting up the card in between jerks. Continue until you've formed circular fan shapes (see photo 4). Badger with the dry brush and let dry.

9. Reattach any hardware you removed from the box.

Photo 3

Photo 4

Harvest Home Stencilled Chair

YOU'LL USE READY-MADE STENCILS TO CREATE TRADITIONAL, COLORED MOTIFS ON A CHAIR PAINTED SATIN BLACK. THE CHAIR SHOWN IS SIMILAR TO THE FAMOUS "HITCHCOCK CHAIR" MANUFACTURED BY LAMBERT HITCHCOCK IN NINETEENTH-CENTURY CONNECTICUT. YOU CAN ADAPT THE INSTRUCTIONS TO ANY CHAIR WITH HORIZONTAL BACK RAILS AND TURNED LEGS AND STRETCHERS.

JEAN TOMASO MOORE,
Designer

MATERIALS

– Wooden chair
– Interior-grade, latex acrylic wood primer
– Interior-grade, latex acrylic, satin finish paint in black
– Stencils of early American motifs, including a basket containing fruits, vegetables, and flowers, a small scroll design, and a small tulip motif*
– Acrylic craft paints in metallic pure gold and metallic antique gold, and in muted red, yellow ocher, light red oxide or pumpkin, lavender, grape, deep purple, and light, medium, and dark greens
– Acrylic latex, satin finish varnish
  *Available at craft stores. Select stencils that will fit the areas of the chair that you plan to decorate.

TOOLS AND SUPPLIES

– Steel wool in 00 grade, or 400-grit sandpaper
– Tack cloth
– Foam brushes in various sizes
– Tape measure
– Scissors
– Tracing paper
– Pencil
– Black poster board
– Painter's tape
– Waxed paper
– Paper towels
– Stencil brush, ⅜ or ½ inch (9.5 mm to 1.3 cm)
– Liquid detergent or brush cleaner
– Small detail brush

INSTRUCTIONS

1. Use the steel wool or sandpaper to lightly sand the chair, removing any old surface paint or finish. Use the tack cloth to clean off any residue.

2. Use a foam brush to apply the latex primer to the chair. Let dry, then apply several coats of the black satin finish paint, allowing each coat of paint to dry between applications.

3. Measure all areas of the chair that you plan to stencil, then select stencil patterns that will fit. If the patterns are contained on one large sheet, cut the smaller patterns from the larger sheet to make them easier to work with.

4. Lay the tracing paper over an area of the chair you plan to stencil. Pencil an outline of the area onto the tracing paper, creating a pattern for a template. Cut out the tracing paper pattern and transfer it to the black poster board. Repeat the process to make multiple poster board templates of all the areas to be stencilled. At this point, experiment with applying colors through your poster board templates onto a sheet of paper (see step 6 for technique), then tape the painted paper on the chair to see how it looks. The stencilled motifs shown in photos 1, 2, and 3 used the following colors: light and dark gold for the large basket; lavender, grape, and yellow for the flowers in the basket; light, medium, and dark green for the leaves; red for the apples; dark purple and yellow or light green for the grapes; light and dark gold for the scroll designs; red, yellow, and green for the individual flowers.

5. Use the painter's tape to attach the templates to the chair. Lay the chair on its back on the work surface. Center the main stencil of the fruit and vegetable basket on the chair back. Use the tape to secure the stencil in place.

6. Squeeze small amounts of one color family onto a piece of the waxed paper: the light, medium, and dark greens for the leaves, for example. Use the lightest hue first, tapping the stencil brush into the paint and working the color into the brush by rotating the brush on the waxed paper. Remove excess paint with a dry paper towel. Apply the paint with a pouncing or tapping motion, holding the almost-dry brush upright against the leafy areas of the stencil. Use a circular swirling motion with the brush to work the color into the areas.

7. Moisten another paper towel and work the brush against it to remove any remaining paint. Load the brush with the medium green paint and, once again, go over the leaf openings. Repeat the process of removing the excess paint. When the brush is clear and the previous color is dry on the chair, highlight the leaves using the darkest hue of the green paint. Layering colors in this manner helps to create shading and a more natural looking design.

8. Apply all colors as in steps 6 and 7. To prevent color from spilling into unwanted areas of the stencil, use the painter's tape to mask the areas. When drastically changing color values, from green to purple or red to yellow, for example, either use a separate brush for each color family, or wash the brush out with soapy water and dry before reusing.

9. When using a design element that is directional such as the tulip on both the right and left sides of the chair, create a symmetrical look by painting the design one way, then cleaning all the paint off the stencil and flipping it over on the other side.

10. To apply paint to leg turnings or carvings on the chair, use the painter's tape to mask off each side of the turning to create an even stripe. Use the small detail brush to apply the gold paint between the tape. Pull the tape off each area before the paint is dry to help maintain a cleaner line.

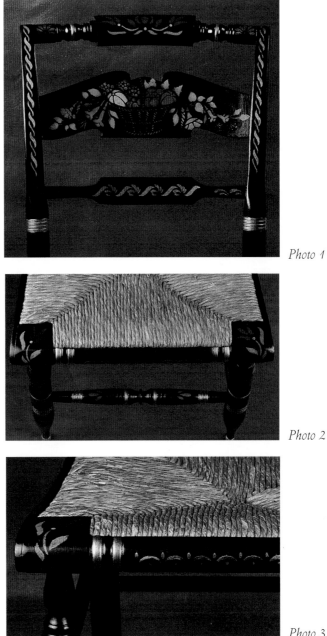

Photo 1

Photo 2

Photo 3

11. When all designs have been applied to the chair, allow the paint to cure for 24 to 72 hours. When the painted surface is completely dry and set, use a foam brush to apply several thin coats of the acrylic latex satin varnish, allowing each coat to dry between applications.

scrimshaw

Throughout the Pacific and also in Nantucket and New Bedford and Sag Harbor, you will come across lively sketches of whales and whaling scenes, graven by the fishermen themselves on Sperm-Whale teeth, or ladies busks wrought out of the Right-Whale bone and other like skrimshander articles, as the whalemen call the numerous little ingenious contrivances they elaborately carve out of the tough material in their hours of ocean leisure. Some of them have little boxes of dentistical looking implements, specially intended for the skrimshandering business. But, in general, they toil with their jack-knives alone, and, with that almost omnipotent tool of the sailor, they will turn you out anything you please in the way of a mariner's fancy.

Herman Melville, *Moby Dick; or, The Whale,* 1851

Watch Stand, Charles B. Toby; 1819, Cape Horn, Chile. Bone, baleen, wood, paper, metal. 8⁵/₁₆ x 3¹/₂ x 2¹/₃ inches (21.1 x 8.9 x 5.4 cm). From the collections of The Mariners' Museum, Newport News, Va.

It's hard to imagine that the delicate and fantastically detailed objects we call scrimshaw were the byproducts of one of eighteenth- and nineteenth-century America's most grueling industries: the hunting of whales on the open seas, and the manufacture of oil from their fat on board ship. No one knows the true origin of the word *scrimshaw*. Some researchers think it derives from a Dutch expression meaning "a lazy fellow." Others think it came from the prototypical Yankee word "scrimp," which describes economizing by the use of humble and frugal materials (including all the scrap parts of a whale), and the words "shaw" or "shand," referring to sawing or sanding.

Although today we use alternative fuels and protect many whale species, between the American Revolution and the Civil War, whale oil was the preferred fuel for lamps, and was considered an excellent lubricant for machinery. To meet the demand for oil, whalers set out from New England ports on voyages that lasted up to four years. The industry peaked in the mid-1840s, when more than 700 ships comprised the American whaling fleet. Sailors' lives alternated between long hours of tedium, and frenetic, frightening chases once a whale was sighted. After a kill, the animal was hauled aboard, butchered, and oil rendered from its fat.

Making scrimshaw was one way sailors filled hours of boredom. Some sailors engraved a record of their experiences on whale teeth, including the "Nantucket sleigh ride," the life-threatening moment when a harpooned whale tried to escape, and dragged the sailors and their harpoon boat behind, sometimes for miles.

The two species most prized were the sperm whale (Melville's famous Moby Dick) and the right whale (so named because it floats on its side after being killed). After rendering, the leftovers comprised the raw materials of scrimshaw: whalebone; the dark gray baleen of the right whale, which the animal uses to strain its food from sea water; and the lower jaw and ivory teeth of the sperm whale. One medium-sized sperm whale has a 20-foot (6m) jaw and fifty 4- to 10-inch-long (10.2 to 25.4 cm) teeth, some 4 or 5 pounds (1.8 to 2.2 kg) each.

Scrimshanders used simple tools for their craft, and frequently improvised from materials at hand. Implements included saws and files fabricated from barrel hoops, sharkskin "sandpaper," sailcloth needles, and the ubiquitous jackknife. The sailors often gathered for their own equivalent of a quilting bee.

Whalebone is stronger and more durable than wood and feels better in the hand. Scrimshanders used whalebone and ivory to make just about every tool needed on board, including tools for carpentry, sail making, and rope making. They also used their time to make canes, boxes, sewing and knitting implements, kitchen tools, and personal adornments for their mothers, wives, and sweethearts back home. Most of the finest examples date after 1825, when there was a significant expansion in the American mercantile fleet to compete in world trade (and therefore more sailors on more ships).

Watch Stand (detail), Charles B. Toby; 1819, Cape Horn, Chile. Bone, baleen, wood, paper, metal. 8⁵⁄₁₆ x 3½ x 2⅓ inches (21.1 x 8.9 x 5.4 cm). From the collections of The Mariners' Museum, Newport News, Va.

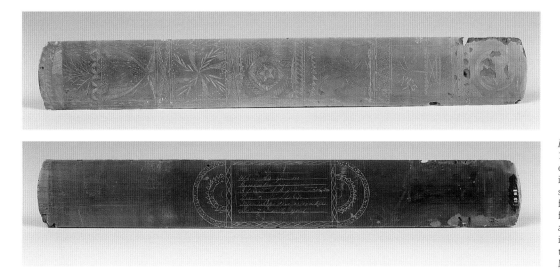

Busk, artist unknown; ca. 1840-1934. Baleen corset busk, engraved with the following inscription: "To __/when this you see/remember me/A friend & A friend will be/give to friendship/friendship[s] due/remember Me and I will you." 13 x 1¾ x ⅛ inches (33 x 4.4 x .3 cm). From the collections of The Mariners' Museum, Newport News, Va.

Sperm Whale Tooth, artist unknown; ca. 1900-1935. Ivory, ink. Length: 5 inches (12.7 cm). From the collections of The Mariners' Museum, Newport News, Va.

The pie crimper or jagging wheel was a commonly made piece of scrimshaw. Familiar to cooks, the crimper's fluted wheel was used to put a fluted edge on pies and pastry crusts, while the wheel could cut strips and shapes from dough. Strong, flexible balleen was the perfect material for making corset busks like the ones shown on page 25, and busks were also made from lighter-colored bone.

Assorted sailor's handiwork, clockwise from top: ditty bag, pie jagger, nineteenth-century hair comb. From the collections of The Mariners' Museum, Newport News, Va.

Many scrimshaw objects not only performed specific functions, they were also an opportunity for their makers' fancy to take full flight! In addition to carvings of incredible detail, some scrimshaw was decorated with engravings colored by rubbing with lampblack and a varnish fixative, combinations of different kinds of bone, or inlaid materials. Some sailors copied magazine illustrations by pasting them on a whale tooth, piercing the outlines with an awl, then removing the paper and connecting the dots. The watch holder pictured on page 24 is a superb example of how magnificent the results can be when scrimshaw materials are combined.

The introduction of petroleum-based fuels and the disruptions of the American Civil War contributed to the decline of the whaling industry, and by the dawn of the twentieth century, it was a thing of the past. Only the glorious artifacts of scrimshaw remain, a testament to the skill and care of the unknown men who made them.

Right: Jagging Wheel, artist unknown; date unknown. Pie crimper made of whale ivory and metal. 6½ x 1¾ inches (16.5 x 4.4 cm). From the collections of The Mariners' Museum, Newport News, Va.

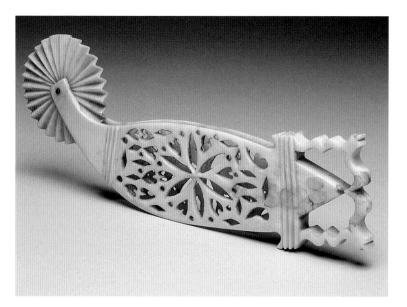

scrimshaw Letter openers

Don't worry, no whales are harmed in the making of this project! These handy letter openers are charming, colorful adaptations of the time-honored folk art of scrimshaw. You'll learn techniques to carve, incise, and color baked polymer clay instead of ivory.

Irene Semanchuk Dean, Designer

Materials

– 1 ounce (28 gm) each of polymer clay in white and beige**
– Metal letter opener*
– Patterns on page 138
– Acrylic paint in black, red, green, and yellow
  *available at office supply stores
  **The beige clay will be used to tint the white clay, and you'll have extra left over.

Tools and Supplies

– Sealable plastic bag
– Dishpan
– Waxed paper
– Rubber printer's brayer or straight-sided drinking glass
– Heat-resistant PVA glue
– Craft knife with a sharp blade
– Ruler
– Oven
– Oven thermometer
– Wet/dry sandpaper, 400, 600, and 800 grit*
– Wet/dry sandpaper, 320 grit* (optional)
– Tracing paper
– Soft leaded pencil or carbon paper
– Sharp pencil or stylus
– Masking tape
– Coaster or folded paper towel
– Cotton swabs
– Toothpicks
– Paper towels
– Needle or pin (optional)
– Piece of denim fabric, or cotton buffing wheel with bench grinder or jeweler's grinder
  *Available at auto supply stores

Instructions

1. First, you'll need to condition the clays. Warm them by sealing them in the plastic bag, then put the bag in the dishpan filled with warm water. Let the bag warm for 10 to 15 minutes. Remove the clays from the bag, and condition each clay separately by rolling it into a long snake, folding it two times, and rolling it back out. Avoid getting air bubbles into the clay, and continue the process until the clay stretches and sags when you pull it apart.

2. Tint the white clay by working a small amount of the beige clay into the white to make an ivory color you find pleasing. Working on a piece of waxed paper, use the brayer to roll the clay into a flat sheet ⅛ inch (3 mm) thick.

3. Coat the handle of the letter opener with the PVA glue and let dry.

4. Use the craft knife and ruler to cut a straight edge on the sheet of clay. Place the handle of the letter opener onto the clay, parallel to and about ¼ inch (6 mm) away from the edge. If the letter opener has a hole in the top, fill the hole with a tiny piece of clay. Wrap the clay around the handle, cutting the sheet of clay so that the edges butt together. Smooth the seam with your fingertips, making the clay as smooth as possible with your fingers or the brayer. Cut excess clay from the top, and use your fingertips to smooth the clay into a pleasing shape. Cut excess clay from the bottom of the handle.

5. Bake the letter opener in the oven at 275°F (135°C) for one hour. It's important that you use the oven thermometer to ensure an accurate baking temperature. Let the clay cool completely. (You'll also want to bake a scrap piece of clay to use as a practice piece when you start carving.)

6. Wet the 400-grit wet/dry sandpaper, and use it to smooth the polymer clay handle. (If there are bumps and larger imperfections, sand first with a coarser sandpaper, such as 320 grit.)

7. Use the pencil and tracing paper to trace the patterns of your choice from page 138. Transfer the designs to the handle by rubbing soft pencil on the reverse side of the tracing paper, or by placing a piece of carbon paper, carbon side down, between the traced design and the handle surface. Use the masking tape to hold everything in place, then use the pencil or stylus to firmly but carefully trace over the lines, transferring the carbon to the clay. Remove the tape.

8. Hold the craft knife in a "backward" position with the tip down but the blade facing away from you. Practice carving on the scrap piece of baked clay, placing it on the coaster or folded paper towel to ease turns and rotations. Slowly pull the tip of the blade towards you, pressing hard enough to make an indentation in the clay. To carve curves, move the handle in the direction of the curve rather than trying to curve the blade's movement. When you feel ready, scribe the handle pattern, avoiding piercing the clay to the metal handle.

9. Carve all of the black lines and outlines first, taking frequent breaks. Use the tip of the blade to carve crosshatched lines, i.e., closely spaced parallel lines, topped with others at right angles to the first. When carving, remember that more vibrant colors are achieved with deeper lines, as well as with more closely spaced crosshatching. If you'd like a color to be more subtle, carve lines only in one direction instead of crosshatching. Crosshatching can also create the illusion of shadows when applied to part of a design. Experiment on your scrap piece to explore different effects.

10. Use a cotton swab to rub black paint into the crosshatching, wiping off the excess with a paper towel. After completing all the black areas, use the 400-grit sandpaper to lightly wet-sand the area, removing excess paint and any nubs of clay created by the draw of the blade. If you lose part of the design from oversanding, recarve it and paint it again.

11. Now you'll carve the lines or crosshatching for colored areas. Because the colored areas are fewer than the black areas, you'll use the tip of a toothpick to apply the paint more precisely into the carved lines. Dab, don't wipe, any excess paint with a paper towel, to avoid smearing color into an unwanted area. Work with one color at a time, starting with darker colors and finishing with the lightest color.

12. If desired, use a needle or pin to add tiny, decorative holes (they can also serve as "berries" on the tree pattern). Use a toothpick to fill the holes with a tiny amount of paint, and dab off the excess.

13. After applying the final color of paint, let dry for an hour. Wet-sand the entire handle, working from 400 up through 800 grit. Rinse and dry.

14. Buff the handle gently with the denim cloth, or use the cotton buffing wheel attached to a bench grinder or jeweler's buffer.

Basketmaking

I found the hoe by the well-house and an old splint basket at the woodshed door, and also found my way down to the field....There is all the pleasure that one can have in gold—the riches of a good hill of potatoes. I longed to go on; but it did not seem frugal to dig any longer after my basket was full, and at last I took my hoe by the middle and lifted the basket to go back up the hill. I was sure that Mrs. Blackett must be waiting impatiently to slice the potatoes into the chowder, layer after layer, with the fish.

Sarah Orne Jewett, *The Country of the Pointed Firs*, 1896

Basketmaking is America's oldest hand-craft, and it remains a vibrant craft practiced by families of artisans and individual enthusiasts nationwide. The earliest known examples in the world are 9,000-year-old Native American basket fragments found in Danger Cave in Utah. European settlers and African slaves brought their own craft techniques to this country and adapted them to local materials. In turn, some Native American tribes adopted these newly-imported techniques! Basketmaking forms and techniques have always depended on the use of indigenous materials like grasses, cane, branches, twigs, and bark—whatever was pliable enough to be coiled, twisted, or

Sewing Basket, artist unknown, Northeastern United States; c. 1920. Ash splint, red dye, wood: h. 5¾ in. (14.6 cm) w. 13½ in. (34.3 cm) diameter. Collection of the Museum of American Folk Art, New York; gift of Judith A. Jedlicka in memory of Robert Bishop. 1991.28.01

woven into strong containers. A few simple hand tools for cutting, splitting, and shaping the material were also needed.

Very broadly categorized, there are two main techniques of basketmaking. Either thin, flat splints of wood or another material are woven together, or grasses or similar materials are coiled and stitched together. The choice of material and density of weave are chosen according to the basket's intended function: a cheese basket needs an openwork weave for draining curds, for example, while a wrapped coil is perfect for making a wide, flat fanner basket for tossing rice in the air to sift out the chaff.

In the 1800s, the European colonists preferred making baskets from wood splint, and in New England it was common to paint them in solid colors. In the Northeast, splint is still predominantly made from the ash tree; in the South, from white oak. While a felled tree is still green, it's split vertically into

sections. After the bark is removed, the craftsperson starts a splint in the wood with a knife, then tears off the splint (also called *riving*) horizontally in the same direction as the grain. A knife or a smoothing tool called a *spokeshave* is then used to smooth the splint. Basketmakers used "crooked knives" to cut and shape splint; the blade was attached to the handle at an angle, which gave the knives their name.

Top left: Square to Round Shopper, Wendy G. Jensen; 1999. Rattan, reed: h. 16 in. (40.6 cm) w. 12 in. (30.5 cm). This basket was inspired by a Native American ash basket that combined a woven square and split uprights completed by a bowl shape. Photo by artist

Top Right: Market Basket, Judy Bryson Quinn; 2000. Reed, twisted seagrass, oil stain: h. 12 in. (30.5 cm) w. 8 in. (20.3 cm) d. 16 in. (40.6 cm). Photo by Kathryn Shaffer

Left: Mending Basket, Wendy G. Jensen; 2000. Rattan: h. 16 in. (40.6 cm) w. 14 in. (35.6 cm). The Taconic basketmakers of New York frequently used this design in their ash splint baskets. Photo by artist.

Below: "Turtle Rib" Basket with Braid, Cynthia W. Taylor; 2000. Handsplit white oak: h. 10 in. (25.4 cm) w. 13 in. (33 cm) d. 9½ in. (24.1 cm). The maker was inspired by styles and techniques of old Southern Appalachian baskets. The piece incorporates wide, tapering ribs extending above the rim, giving the form its "turtle" nickname. Photo by Paul Jeremias.

Several northeastern Native American tribes adopted the splint method from the colonists, adding designs either painted or stamped with stamps cut from potatoes or other tuber vegetables. In the 1800s, they even started making baskets with traditional European shapes to sell to tourists. They added fancy decorations to trinket or sewing baskets to appeal to Victorian tastes, using dyed splint or protruding weave structures. Other tribes in Louisiana and North Carolina made their own versions of splint work. It was also common for Southeastern tribes to make baskets with twill weave, in which the horizontal splits are passed over two or more vertical elements before they are passed under two or more.

The Shakers came to America in 1772 and established settlements in the Northeast, Midwest, and South. A religious sect that stressed the values of self-sufficiency, handwork, simplicity, and practicality, they are famous for the superbly crafted and elegantly formed objects they made. They wove ash or hickory splint over wooden forms to create baskets which were well known and highly desirable as early as the 1840s.

Off the coast of Cape Cod, on Nantucket Island from 1856 to 1892, another distinctive and famous type of basket was made by the keepers of a lightship that was moored off the island's coast to warn passing ships to keep clear. They made the baskets for extra income and to fill the long hours and months of isolation. The Nantucket lightship basket is made with a wooden bottom, a modification used by Nantucket farmers to strengthen baskets. The ribs are set into the bottom like barrel staves. Imported rattan (introduced by whalers who returned from

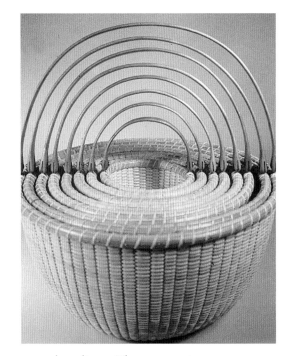

the Pacific) was very tightly woven around circular or (less common) oval molds, and swing-style handles were added. The baskets were frequently made as nested sets.

In the southern Appalachian Mountains that span several states in the southeastern U.S., white oak ribbed baskets were frequently constructed with two flat hoops that crossed at a right angle to form the handle and rim or spine. Thin, round wood strips spread at an angle from the spine to support horizon-

tally woven oak splints. The supporting strips often swooped out to form the region's well-known "buttocks" bottom. Since the late 1800s and early 1900s, melon-shaped baskets such as the fine example on page 34 have proved to be a characteristic form. A very strong, vibrant tradition of white oak basketmaking continues in southern Appalachia, with knowledge passed down within families from generation to generation.

Baskets of coiled, stitched grasses and the needles of pine trees have been made all over the world. The earliest American baskets were made in the Southwest by the people archeologists now call the Basket Makers, the ancient predecessors of the Anasazi and Pueblo people. Their baskets were coiled and stitched, and frequently adorned with striking geometric patterns. The coiling technique characterizes Southwestern baskets,

"Braidy Melon" Basket, Aaron Yakim; 2000. Handsplit white oak: h. 15 in. (38.1 cm) w. 15 in. (38.1 cm) d. 15 in. (38.1 cm). Inspired by the traditional melon-shaped rib baskets of the Southern Appalachians, the maker embellished this piece with his own innovations including alternating flat and round ribs and sapwood braids. Photo by Paul Jeremias

Ginger Jar, Alma P. Hemmings; early 1960s. Pine needles: h. 8 in. (20.3 cm) w. 7 in. (17.8 cm). Photo by Evan Bracken

ket form with them. A fanner is a flat basket used for winnowing chaff from rice. The slaves' descendants, most notably the Gullahs of coastal South Carolina and the sea islands of Georgia, continue to create some of this country's finest coiled baskets, made from bulrushes, palmetto, and a slender wild grass called sweetgrass. The only tool used is a "bone," a spoon with its bowl removed and end sharpened, which is used to pierce the coils so a palmetto strip can bind them in place. The baskets have been sold to the tourist trade since the 1930s, but development is endangering the marshland habitats of the grass.

Native Americans in the Southeast (the Florida Seminoles, and the Coushatta, a tribe originating in Alabama that migrated to Georgia, Florida, and Louisiana) originally used swamp cane to make baskets, but as land was settled and turned to farming, the sources of material declined and they substituted pine needles. We aren't certain when Anglo-Americans began making pine needle baskets, but in 1917 a North Carolina educator credited Mrs. M.J. McAfee of Georgia with the "first" pine needle handcraft. She made a coiled pine needle hat in an effort to provide necessities for her family during the American Civil War. It's possible she learned the technique from slaves in her state, or knew of local Native American craft. Ironically, some Native American tribes were taught pine needle craft in handicraft programs sponsored by the Bureau of Indian Affairs, and they now make contemporary baskets for sale.

Pennsylvania Dutch baskets also utilized coiled straw techniques originating in German culture; German craftsmen in southern Pennsylvania and Virginia made coiled rye straw baskets that were both nailed and lashed together with thin strips of wood.

which are made of willow or yucca. Thin fibers are sewn or woven around fixed horizontal circles or hoops.

Artisans from west central and southern Africa not only brought their own coiled basketry traditions when they came to America as slaves, they also brought the fanner bas-

Reed Bread Basket

This delightful basket not only holds bread, it's the perfect size for a standard box of tissues, compact discs, or #10 envelopes. These directions are written for right-handed people, so you'll need to reverse them if you're a southpaw.

Wendy Gadbois Jensen,
Designer

MATERIALS

– ³/₄-inch (1.9 cm) flat reed*, five 22-inch (55.9 cm) pieces and nine 17-inch (43.2 cm) pieces, for base stakes and uprights
– ¹/₄-inch (6 mm) flat oval reed*, for weavers (the elements you'll weave around the stakes) and lasher (the element that lashes the rim to the basket) Use dyed reed for the accents shown in the photo, if desired.
– ³/₈-inch (9.5 mm) flat reed*, for creating the last row of weaving (false rim)
– ¹/₂-inch (1.3 cm) flat oval reed*, for inner and outer rims
– ³/₈-inch (9.5 mm) half round reed*, two 11-inch (27.9 cm) pieces, for handles (optional)
  *Available in "hanks" containing approximately 1 pound (0.454 kg) of one size of reed. You'll have material left over to create 2 more baskets, if you wish.

TOOLS AND SUPPLIES

– Dishpan or bucket
– Pencil
– Measuring tape
– Scissors
– Utility knife
– Awl
– 2 size 8 knitting needles
– Piece of string (optional)
– Spring-type clothespins
– Sandpaper

INSTRUCTIONS

Making the Base
1. Soak the 14 flat reed base stakes and the six ¹/₄-inch (6 mm) flat oval weavers for five minutes in the dishpan filled with warm water.

2. Reed has a right and wrong side. The right side is the smoother side, and when you bend it, tiny splinters will stand up from the wrong side. Use the pencil and measuring tape to mark the centers on the wrong sides of one 22-inch (55.9 cm) and one 17-inch (43.2 cm) base stake.

3. On a flat surface, lay out the five 22-inch base stakes horizontally in front of you, wrong side up, ends even, and place the marked stake in the center. Leave a ³/₈-inch (9.5 mm) gap between the stakes. Weight them on the left end with the scissors.

4. Take the 17-inch (43.2 cm) marked stake (A) and begin weaving it, wrong side up, over the horizontal base stakes. Pass it over the horizontal stake closest to you then under the next one, continuing the over-under pattern, called a plain weave, across the horizontal stakes (fig. 1). Position stake A so it crosses the center-marked horizontal stake.

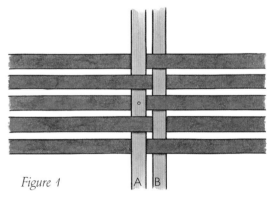

Figure 1   A B

5. Refer to figure 2. Position stake B about ³/₈ (9.5 mm) inch to the right of stake A. Weave stake B under horizontal stake 1, then over and under stakes 2, 3, 4, and 5. Weave

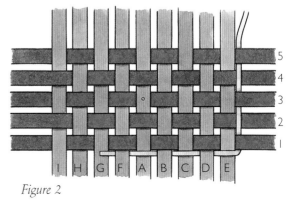

Figure 2

in stakes C, D, and E, wrong side up, maintaining a ³/₈-inch (9.5 mm) gap between the vertical and horizontal stakes, and ensuring the ends are even.

6. Remove the scissors and weave in the remaining 17-inch base stakes F, G, H, and I. The basket base is now finished, its inside facing up. It should measure roughly 9³/₄ (24.8 cm) inches long by 5³/₈ (13.65 cm) inches wide. The squares of space between stakes should be consistent.

Turning up the Basket Sides
1. To help turn up the basket sides, you'll now crease the stakes around the base's edge. Working one stake at a time, put your finger on the stake at the edge of the base, lift up the stake with your opposing hand to crease the piece, and make a hard fold upward. Some cracking is normal. These bent stakes are called *uprights*.

2. Take one of the ¹/₄-inch (6 mm) flat oval weavers and determine its flat (wrong) side, which will face the inside of the basket. Again referring to figure 2, position one end of the weaver toward the left of the basket, on top of an upright, on the long side of the basket closest to you. The long end of the weaver should extend to the right, parallel to stake 1.

3. Refer to figure 3. Using the over-under plain weave, weave over and under each upright, one at a time, pushing the weaver snugly against the base as you work toward

Figure 3

the basket's right-hand corner. To maintain the correct tension of the weaver and obtain the desired basket shape, keep the uprights evenly spaced, and in the position and angle

desired for the finished basket (both side to side and inward and outward). As you weave, there should be hardly any tension on the weaver. Too much tension causes the sides to slope inward and the uprights to crowd together; watch the corners in particular, as they tend to lean inward first.

4. Continue weaving around the basket until you reach the beginning of the weaver. To end the row, continue to weave, overlapping the beginning of the row for four uprights (see fig. 3), then cut the weaver with the utility knife. There should be no ends protruding from the inside or outside of the basket.

5. Start the second row of weaving on the basket's opposing, long side, keeping the weaver's flat side up. The weave should also be opposite the first row, i.e., if the weaver went over an upright on the first row then the weaver should go behind (or under) the upright on the second row. To keep the basket strong, remember to pack, or push, the rows of weaving together, leaving no space between them. After weaving one long side, lift the entire side of the basket and crease it upward to help begin the shaping. Continue around the corner, standing up the corner uprights to get the correct tension of the weaver. Weave around until you reach the beginning of the row. Lap the weaver over four more uprights, and cut it. The basket's rectangular shape will begin to appear.

6. Turn the basket on its side on the table. Start the third row of weaving on the same side as row one, working from the outside of the basket. The beginning end of the weaver should be on the outside of the basket, with the weaver's rounded side facing out.

7. If you wish to achieve the color combination of reed shown in the photograph, follow this sequence of weavers:

– 4 rows of natural ¼-inch (6 mm) flat oval reed
– 2 rows of dyed ¼-inch (6 mm) flat oval reed
– 1 row of natural ¼-inch (6 mm) flat oval reed
– 2 rows of dyed ¼-inch (6 mm) flat oval reed
– 4 rows of natural ¼-inch (6 mm) flat oval reed
– 1 row of natural ⅜-inch (9.5 mm) flat reed

Remember to alternate sides to begin a row. If you don't use dyed reed, simply weave 13 rows of plain weave. Then weave one more row of the ⅜-inch (9.5 mm) flat reed for the final, top row, which will be sandwiched between the rims.

8. If the upright tops are dry, turn the basket over in the warm water and soak for a couple of minutes to soften them.

9. Refer to figure 4. Starting at any point along the top of the basket, crease every other upright, folding them toward the inside of the basket. Crease them as close to the last row of weaving as possible; some cracking will occur. Cut off the uncreased uprights as close to the last row of weaving as possible. Cut the creased uprights to resemble a picket fence about 1½ inches (3.8 cm) above the basket body. Fold each upright to the inside over the first row of weaving, then tuck it under the remaining rows of weaving by running the awl or knitting needle under the rows of weaving, moving the awl to one side, and sliding in the upright. The basket body is now completed.

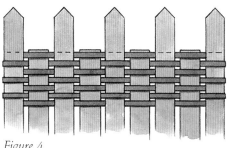

Figure 4

Making the Side Handles

1. Soak the two pieces of ⅜-inch (9.5 mm) half round reed in warm water for 10 min-utes. With the flat side to the inside of the curve, gently but firmly bend one reed, starting from one end and working your way to the other. Holding the ends of the handle about 2 inches apart in one hand, place the handle on the two uprights that flank the center upright on one end of the basket. The handle should be about 1½ inches (3.8 cm) above the top of the basket; make a pencil mark on the outside of the handle where it meets the top of the basket.

2. Relax the handle ends. Refer to figure 5. Use the ruler to measure ½ inch (1.3 cm) below the mark, and make a second mark. Lay the flat sides of both handles together and make identical marks on the second handle. Lay the handles on a cutting board and use the utility knife to cut straight down into the marks, ⅛ inch (3 mm) deep, then gently twist the blade toward the notch to pop out the piece. Repeat for the other notch.

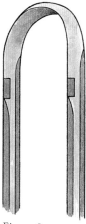

Figure 5

3. Now you'll thin the area below the notch so the handle can be tucked into the basket's side. Starting directly below the notch, cut away some of the material to form a flat surface. To flatten the handle's back side (which will lie against an upright), start about ¾ inch (1.9 cm) above the notch and cut away material, moving toward the handle end. Be careful not to cut away too much, especially near the notch. Taper the handle's other leg. Repeat steps 1 through 3 to make the second handle.

4. Now you'll insert a handle at each end of the basket, on the two uprights to either side of the center upright. Refer to figure 6.

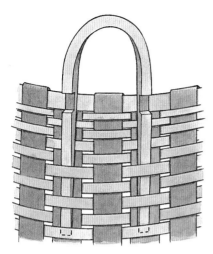

Figure 6

Counting from the top, insert one knitting needle between the seventh row of weaving and the first upright. Repeat with the second needle and the second upright. Slide the needles down under the weaving to the base and over to one side. While supporting the (weaker) notched areas with your thumb and index finger, form the handle into a U shape. Slide both legs down into the spaces at the same time until the notches are directly over the top row of weaving. If desired, secure the handle with string until the rims are in place. Remove the needles and install the second handle.

Attaching the Basket Rims

1. Measure the basket's top outer circumference. Cut the ¹/₂-inch (1.3 cm) flat oval reed for the outer rim 4 inches longer than this measurement, and the inner rim 2 inches (5.1 cm) longer. With flat sides together, soak the rims in warm water for 10 minutes. To fit them in the dishpan, you can coil them in the direction they'll fit on the basket, with the shorter rim on the inside to help "train" the material.

2. Holding the rims in your right hand, and starting on the long side closest to you, use the clothespins to attach the outer rim to the outside of the top row and the inner rim to the inside. Start the rim ends 4 inches (10.2 cm) from each other, with the flat sides against the weaving. Wrap the rims around the basket in a counter clockwise direction, pushing the rims into the corners and placing the outer rim into the handle notches. Use a clothespin every 5 inches (12.7 cm) and near every corner. When you're back to where you started, lap the ends over the starting points.

3. Now you'll *scarf,* or thin, the overlapping ends so that, when placed together, they're as thick as one piece of ¹/₂-inch (1.3 cm) flat oval rim. Use the pencil to mark the length of the overlap on the rim pieces. For the outside rim, make a mark on the underlying rim, where the end lies, and on the back of the top piece, at the beginning point. Repeat for the inner rim. Remove the rims from the basket.

4. Refer to figure 7. Working at an angle and between the pencil marks, use the knife to remove half of the material from the flat side (or back) of the rim end lying on top, and half of the material from the rounded side (or front) of the rim's starting point. When finished, round the rim ends, sand for a more finished look, and re-pin the rims to the basket. The rim should cover only the top row of weaving.

Lashing the Basket

1. To secure the rims and handles, you'll use a method similar to an overcast stitch. Lash-

Photo 1

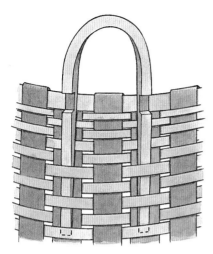

Figure 7

ing must be as snug as possible. This basket has a double lash: the lasher travels once around the basket, then reverses in the opposite direction. Take a piece of ¼-inch (6 mm) flat oval reed about four times the circumference of the basket and soak it in warm water for five minutes. This will be the lasher.

2. Refer to figure 8. To the right of the scarf joints and starting from the outside, anchor the lasher's tail by inserting it (wrong side facing you) inside the inner rim, passing it over the top row of weaving and down inside the outer rim, leaving a ⅜-inch (9.5 mm) tail. Pull the long end of the lasher snug and begin to lash the basket, moving up and to the right. Catch the tail of the lasher

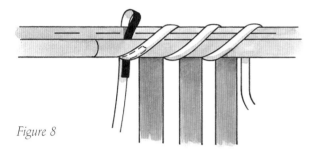

Figure 8

as it moves upward, bringing it over and behind the rim and out the next space between the uprights. Make sure the rims are aligned over the top row of weaving and pulled tight, as shown in photos 2 and 3, and that the lasher catches only the top row of weaving. Maintain the tension by using clothespins to secure the stitch that was just completed. Continue lashing around the basket. At the handles, take the lasher across the outside of the handle, feeding the lasher through the handle and out the next space between the uprights.

3. When the lasher reaches the first stitch, feed the lasher through it again and reverse the direction. Start lashing to the left, using the same spaces as before and creating an "X" atop the rims and on the outside of the handles (fig. 9). Stop lashing before completing the last stitch. To secure the lasher, use the awl to enlarge the space under the first round

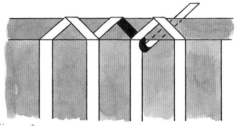

Figure 9

of lashing, and slide the lasher in, down, and to the inside, using the awl to hold the space open if necessary. Proceed carefully so as not to break the lashing. The "X" pattern should still be in place. The lasher should be headed toward the inside of the basket at this point. Refer to figure 10. Bring the lasher down and to the inside, and slide it under the lashing near the space the lasher would have nor-

Figure 10

mally gone through. The pattern of the lashing remains the same. Bring the lasher up between the rims at an angle leaning to the left. Pull the lasher tight and cut it off just below the top edge of the rim.

4. Adjust the shape of the basket while it's still damp by gently but firmly bending the rims into square corners and straight sides. If the basket doesn't sit flat, push up on the bottom and re-crease the edges where the basket begins to turn upward. Let dry, then sand the handles, and use the scissors to trim any hairs.

Photo 2

Photo 3

Pine Needle Basket

Coiled and stitched pine needles are used to make this exquisite basket. You'll want to allow plenty of time to relax and enjoy the process of creating it. Pine needle basketmakers originally used raffia to bind together coiled baskets, but today's craftspeople have the option of using artificial sinew. Finish the basket with old-fashioned, sweet-smelling beeswax, or substitute a coat of shellac, if you prefer.

Judy Mofield Mallow, Designer

MATERIALS

– Pine needles, about ½ pound (224 gm)*
– Artificial sinew, to serve as thread**
  *The basket shown is made of 13 coils, and its base measures 6 inches (15.2 cm) across. The sides are 3 inches (7.6 cm) high and consist of 15 rows. From handle to handle, the basket is 11½ inches (29.2 cm) across.
  **Available from craft and leathercraft stores, and basketry suppliers

TOOLS AND SUPPLIES

– Container for soaking needles
– Towel
– Scissors
– Sewing needle
– Spring-type clothespins
– Needle-nose pliers
– Gauge or a wide drinking straw
– Masking tape
– Waxed paper or newspaper (optional)
– 2 to 4 ounces (56 to 112 gm) of beeswax
– Double boiler
– Foam brush
– Shellac (optional)

INSTRUCTIONS

Preparing the Materials
1. Cover the pine needles with boiling water and let them soak for 30 minutes.

2. Drain the water, and wrap the needles in a towel.

Starting the Center
1. Now you'll make the pine needle knot. As shown in figure 1, choose five to seven of the longest needles and tie them together with sinew just below the caps. Holding both ends, twist the bundle as tightly as you can and tie a knot in the center. Use the scissors to cut off the caps, and pull the two ends together to form one bundle with the loose ends to the left.

2. Thread the sewing needle with 1½ yards (1.35 m) of the sinew, and knot one end. Insert the needle from the back of the knot through the center and out through the front of the knot (fig. 2). Begin taking stitches overlapping the coil, keeping them about ¼ inch (6 mm) apart around the outside edge of the knot. See figures 2 and 3. This will establish the stitching pattern for the rest of the basket. Keep the coil going by adding new needles every 2 to 3 inches (5.1 to 7.6 cm); remove their caps and insert them into the middle of the coil.

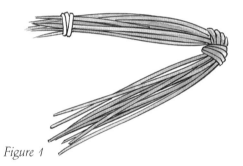

Figure 1

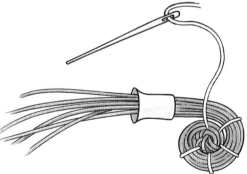

Figure 2

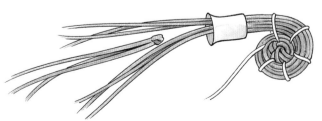

Figure 3

Forming the Bottom

1. After you've come around the pine needle knot with the first stitched coil, start the second coil by adding extra needles, using the gauge or straw to keep the thickness of the coil consistent. Insert the needle through the previous stitches close to the top of the stitch. This creates a split stitch, because the needle is actually splitting the thread. Turn the basket bottom over regularly to check the needle's placement. On the back side, it should be placed in the middle of the stitch, close to the top. The needle should then come out the front in the middle of the same stitch.

2. Continue stitching, coiling, and adding needles until the bottom of the basket is 11 inches (27.9 cm) across or the desired size.

Forming the Basket Sides

1. Place a coil directly on top of the last (outer) row of the bottom and continuing to stitch, adding needles and coiling as before. To make the walls flare outward, position each succeeding coil so it rests just slightly to the outside of the one beneath (fig. 4).

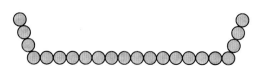

Figure 4

2. A coiled basket's shape is determined by the placement of each coil. Use a piece of tape or colored thread to mark the spot where you went up to make the sides. As you come around to the mark with each new coil, check the basket's shape. If it starts to cup in, push the next coil out a little. Continue until you start the handles.

3. As the basket's diameter increases, you may need to add new stitches between existing stitches to strengthen the sides. There are several ways to add more thread. You can tie new thread on to the existing thread's "tail," then pull the knot into the middle of a coil to hide it. Or, you can run the end of the existing thread down through several coils to secure it, then add new thread to the needle and run it up through several coils, being sure it emerges in exactly the same place where the original thread ended (fig. 5). Either way, it's best to leave thread ends on the outside of the basket until you finish, then trim them off.

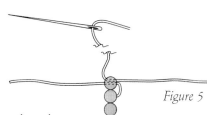

Figure 5

4. To ensure correct placement of the handles, put tape across the inner bottom of the basket and up the sides to the edge of the last coil taken (fig. 6). This will help line up the handles so they're evenly spaced. From the last stitch, start wrapping the sinew around the coil for approximately 4 inches (10.2 cm). Gently bend the coil and attach it to the basket on the other side of the tape.

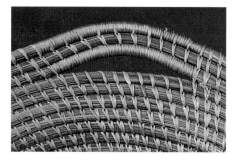

Figure 6

5. Melt the beeswax in a double boiler on top of the stove, then use the brush to coat the basket. It will dry almost instantly, but continue coating both sides. Place the basket in a 200°F (92°C) oven and heat it 15 to 20 minutes until the wax melts into the coils of the basket.

silhouette Art

I built a cottage for Susan and myself....Our parlor, small and neat, was ornamented with our two profiles in one gilt frame, and with shells and pretty pebbles on the mantelpiece...

Nathaniel Hawthorne, "The Village Uncle," from *Twice-Told Tales*, 1837

Silhouette of Man, Silhouette of Woman, Silhouette of Girl, artist unknown, probably New England; c. 1835. Cut paper, watercolor on paper, stamped brassmat, wood frame; left h. 3⅝ inches (9.2 cm) w. 2⅝ inches (6.7 cm); middle h. 3⁵/₁₆ inches (8.4 cm) w. 2⅝ inches (6.7 cm) d. 2⅝ inches (6.7 cm); right h. 3⅜ inches (8.6 cm) w. 2⅛ inches (5.4 cm). Collection of the Museum of American Folk Art, New York; gift of Robert Bishop. 1985.28.2 1985.28.3 1985.28.4

The simplicity of a silhouette belies the art form's remarkable history: silhouette art spans all recorded time and connects many of the world's cultures. By definition, a silhouette is a monochrome composition, dark against light or vice versa, in which the image is bounded by a very sharp outline. Darkened profiles are found on the cave walls of Paleolithic humans. Writings detail the shadow puppetry of ancient Egypt, China, and Turkey. Examples of European silhouette art survive from the seventeenth century, and American settlers brought the craft with them.

Silhouette art was popular in America from 1790 to 1840. During this time, the nation developed a middle class whose members wanted fine art, such as portraits of loved ones. Itinerant and studio silhouette artists rose to meet the demand, offering their creations as inexpensive portraits. Often using only a pair of scissors and a skilled eye, an artist would cut out the subject's profile from black paper within minutes. A good silhouette captured the literal essence of its subject, making the portrait an instant heirloom. Although the camera largely replaced the art of silhouette for making inexpensive portraits, silhouettes have remained cherished.

The word silhouette is French in origin, and is mostly likely a satirical reference to a notoriously tight-fisted and unpopular eighteenth-century finance officer, Etienne de Silhouette. Some researchers believe he may have been a practitioner of the art, but others link his name to a derisive phrase used to describe frugal options: *à la Silhouette*. Silhouettes, being a cheap alternative to portraits, would have been à la Silhouette, as well.

A silhouette can be drawn, painted, or cut out of paper. Silhouette artists sometimes embellished their work with pencil shading or watercolors, as shown on page 44. Early American hand-drawn silhouettes were painted onto ivory, plaster, or glass, and the nineteenth-century American pottery industry started producing porcelain with silhouettes on them in imitation of classical Greek pottery. Silhouette art developed as a pastime, particularly for women, in the nineteenth century. Silhouettes were collected and exchanged in scrap books, and were made in miniature for mounting in rings, brooches, scarf-pins, and pendants. For America's early Quakers, members of the Religious Society of Friends, silhouettes were the only form of portraiture allowed until the late nineteenth century. At the time of the restriction, interpretation of scripture forbade the creation or display of graven images on the grounds that they might be religious idols.

Silhouettes weren't limited to portraits. Artists sometimes rendered detailed scenes in silhouette. *Scheren-schnitten*, the art of cutting designs from paper, is based on the same principles as the silhouette.

Shadowgraphy was another means of making a silhouette. It required less individual talent or artistry by enabling the maker to trace the shadow of a profile. A shadowgraphy machine reduced the sitter's profile to the size of a silhouette. About the size of a cigar box, the machine had a lens glued to a sliding block or frame on one end to use for focusing the image. A mirror in the box reflected the image onto a piece of frosted glass on top, and the craftsman laid a piece of paper on top of the frosted glass and traced the image. Freehand scissor work, cutting the silhouette out of paper (or sometimes cloth) without any preliminary

drawing, is the most challenging and the most common method. Though scissors were invented around 1500 B.C.E., they were not a common domestic tool until the sixteenth century.

Silhouette artists launched their iconic status in American folk art by appearing at a variety of venues: early World's Fairs in Chicago, Dallas, and New York, and seasonal and year-round amusement parks, including Disneyland in California, where silhouette artists still work. A banner reputed to be hung in the booth of a contemporary Midwestern artist suggested professional competitiveness. It read, "$25,000.00 reward to anyone who can cut a silhouette as good and as fast as I can."

Silhouettes of John and Christina Vogler, artist unknown; c. 1825-1830. Collection of Old Salem.

Girl with Baby Carriage, Ann Leslie; 1994. Black paper; h. 4 inches (10.2 cm) w. 5 inches (12.7 cm). Photo by artist

silhouette portrait

You'll be surprised by how easy it is to create an old-fashioned silhouette portrait. Making accurate cuts takes practice. To hone your skills with the scissors, make a silhouette of a subject or two who'll sit patiently and won't criticize your efforts, such as your dog or cat!

Karl Johnson,
Designer

MATERIALS

- 5½ x 8-inch (14 x 20.3 cm) piece of white paper, in a weight thinner than copy paper
- White or off-white 5 x 7-inch (12.7 x 17.8 cm) heavy, white card stock
- Black ink
- Purchased oval picture frame
  *Note: these instructions are for creating one silhouette.

TOOLS AND SUPPLIES

- A subject
- Sharp, thin specialty scissors with a straight cutting surface 1-inch (2.5 cm) long, or surgical scissors
- Scrap of newspaper or drop cloth
- Small artist's paintbrush
- Glue stick

INSTRUCTIONS

1. Seat your subject at a right angle, 3 to 5 feet (1 to 1.5 m) away, and at your eye-level. The subject should sit with a straight back, facing straight ahead, chin perpendicular to the floor. The eyes should be open and the face in repose, with mouth closed and not smiling.

2. Hold the white, lightweight paper softly between two fingers in your non-dominant hand. With practice, you'll discover a posture that suits you.

3. Observe your subject and note the characteristics of his or her profile. Think "bust to back," examining the profile from the chest, up the neck to the chin, lips, nose, eyes, forehead, top of head, back of head,

back of neck, to the upper back. Silhouettes are one continuous line, beginning with the middle of the subject's bust. You want to know where you're going and where you'll end up before you start cutting with the scissors.

4. If you're cutting with your right hand, begin cutting at the lower right corner. If cutting with your left hand, begin cutting at the lower left corner. Begin cutting your subject's profile, moving the paper around the scissors, rather than forcing the scissors through the paper.

5. Decide if you want your mounted silhouette to face left or right. Place the appropriate backside of the cut profile on the newspaper or drop cloth, and use the paintbrush to lightly but thoroughly coat the exposed side with the ink. Allow the ink to dry.

6. Apply the glue stick to the unpainted backside of the cut profile. Place the cut profile, glue side down, in the center of the card stock, smoothing it down with your hands.

7. Place the silhouette in a purchased frame, trimming the white card stock which contains the mounted silhouette to fit.

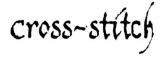

cross~stitch

With her near-sightedness, and those tremulous fingers of hers, at once inflexible and delicate, she could not be a seamstress; although her sampler, of fifty years gone by, exhibited some of the most recondite specimens of ornamental needlework.

Nathaniel Hawthorne, *The House of the Seven Gables,* 1851

Every girl in colonial America had to learn basic sewing skills in order to create and repair the various textile items in her household. In homes that were affluent enough to afford its females some leisure time and money to spend, girls would also learn ornamental needlework, how to decorate textile items and create stitched pictures.

Young children learned basic embroidery stitches. Girls from affluent families who were educated in boarding schools, seminaries, or female academies learned more advanced needlework and embroidery; until the mid-nineteenth century, most schools required their female students to complete a piece of needlework as a graduation requirement.

Moravian Sampler (detail), Christina Spach; 1804. Collection of Old Salem.

In the 1600s and early 1700s, American girls and women created "exemplars," or samplers, which were long, narrow pieces of fabric embroidered with examples of different stitches. The samplers were kept rolled up until they were needed as reference (early English samplers were made and used in the same way). Samplers were not marked with names or dates, and often contained symbols commonly used in Europe, such as stags and fleur-de-lis. Older samplers emphasized the quality of workmanship and stitchery, not the use of realistic color; an animal could be blue, for example.

By the mid-1700s, seamstresses began making a distinctively American sampler. Usually made of homespun linen (sometimes cotton or wool) and stitched with silk or linen thread, the sampler contained embroidered numbers and alphabet letters. Additional decorations might include: a verse or quotations from the Bible; the name of the maker; her birth date; the date she finished the sampler; her town or community; her teacher's name; and images such as landscapes, flowers, animals, or houses. Samplers became squarer in shape, with one or more scenes occupying the center, which was surrounded by symmetrical borders. Showpiece samplers contained a variety of stitches: cross, flat, bullion knot, outline, buttonhole, and satin.

Tulip cross~stitched sampler

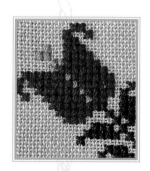

We have the Pennsylvania Dutch to thank for one of American folk art's most beloved motifs, the tulip. This charming little sampler reflects that tradition, and it's an easy project for beginners because it uses only a simple cross-stitch. The directions include instructions for giving the piece a mellow, aged appearance using cold coffee.

Kathy Barrick-Dieter, Designer

MATERIALS AND TOOLS

- 9- x 12-inch (22.9 x 30.5 cm) piece of cream-colored linen with 32 threads per inch (2.5 cm)
- Chalk, straight pins, or thread (optional)
- Scissors
- Embroidery floss in flesh-toned pink, avocado green, mocha brown, and deep red, 1 skein each (you'll have leftovers)
- Tapestry needle in a size suitable for closely woven fabric*
- Embroidery hoop** (optional)
- Iron
- Picture frame, 5 x 7 inches (12.7 x 17.8 cm)
  *Available in craft and sewing supply stores
  **Some cross-stitchers think hoops distort stitches. If you use one, don't leave the fabric in it overnight, or it will stretch permanently.

INSTRUCTIONS

1. There are a few essential tips for making a cross-stitch sampler. As shown in figure 1, work all the upper crossing stitches in the same direction when you take your stitches; stitches that cross in different directions look uneven. You'll save time and thread if you work back and forth across a pattern in rows; slant the lower threads all one way as you stitch in one direction, and slant the upper threads the other way on your return. If you're sewing diagonal rows or scattered, individual stitches, it's best to complete one stitch at a time.

2. Because you're working on linen, you'll make the cross-stitches over two threads of linen vertically and two threads of linen horizontally. Each symbol on the pattern on page 52 represents one cross-stitch in a specific color of embroidery floss; see the key on page 52 for the color codes. For example,

in the chart detail shown in figure 3, the circles represent deep red and the horseshoe a flesh-toned pink. To create the tulip's stamens, count over and down to the point where you'll make one cross stitch in pink. Skip two vertical and two horizontal threads to the right, and make another stitch in pink. Starting down one row, underneath the spot you skipped, make 11 more cross-stitches in pink, stacking one on top of the other. Make four cross-stitches in deep red on both sides of the fourth pink stitch, and so on, taking stitches in red wherever a circle appears on the chart.

3. The 9- x 12-inch (22.9 x 30.5 cm) piece of linen allows a margin of approximately 2¼ inches (5.7 cm) around the sampler. You can begin the sampler in the upper right or lower left corner, or you can center it. To find the center of the linen, fold it in half horizontally, then vertically. Pinch the center corner of the linen tightly. When you open up the linen, the center will be creased. If you wish, mark the centerlines with chalk, straight pins, or basting thread.

4. The chart has arrows indicating the center of the design. Count the stitches on the chart from the center to each edge, and translate the figure onto the linen in terms of threads per stitch. Then you'll know where the edges of the embroidery will fall. For example, you may count 50 stitches (squares) on the chart from the center to the right-hand edge. Since you're making each stitch over two threads of the linen, this means the right-hand edge of the embroidery will fall 100 threads to the right of the center of the fabric.

5. To anchor the first stitch of a new area in the design, leave a 1-inch (2.5 cm) tail of floss dangling free at the back, then catch it under the next few stitches (see fig. 4). As you

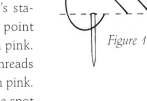

Figure 1

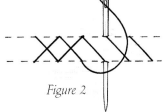

Figure 2

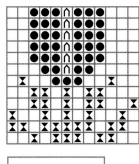

✗	Green
⋒	Pink
●	Red
♥	Brown

Figure 3

Figure 4

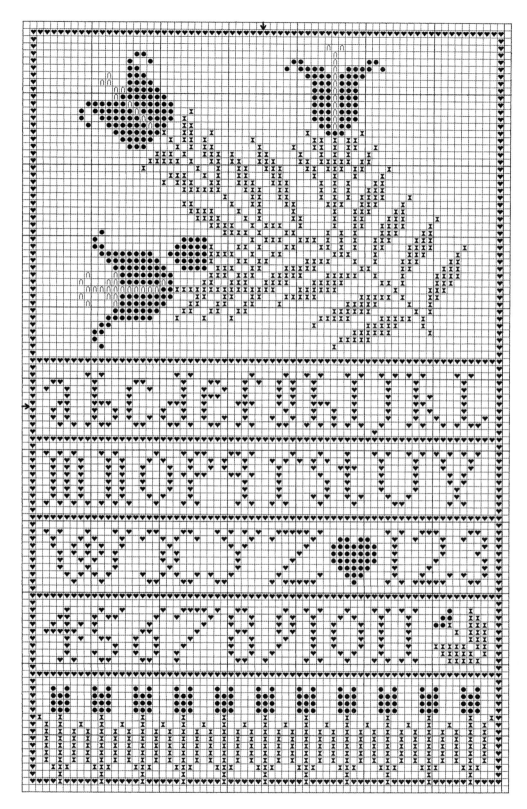

work, you can save floss by not snipping and tying off the floss every time you change color. Instead, take the strand to a distant point in the linen, pull it through to the front, and remove the needle. After you finish stitching the interim color, pull the dangling strand of color number one through to the back, rethread the needle, and weave it through the backs of the newly completed stitches to the point where color number one starts again.

6. After finishing the sampler, you can give it the appearance of age, if desired. Brew a very strong cup of coffee and put it in the refrigerator to chill. Dunk the sampler in the cold coffee, then wring it out and lay it flat to dry. Rub it with a few coffee grounds to add "age" spots, then iron it dry.

7. Install the sampler in the picture frame. If you'd like the fabric of your sampler to last a very long time, let it "breathe" and don't cover it with glass or plastic.

Color Codes

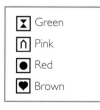

☒	Green
⋂	Pink
●	Red
♥	Brown

Note: The large heart in the pattern is coded for red. Substitute pink thread in the heart if you'd like to achieve the look shown in the photograph on page 50.

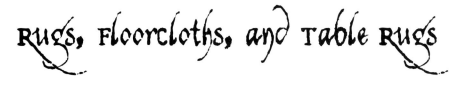

Rugs, Floorcloths, and Table Rugs

It was a mighty nice family, and a mighty nice house, too....The walls of all the rooms were plastered, and most had carpets on the floors, and the whole house was whitewashed on the outside....Colonel Grangerford was a gentleman, you see. He was a gentleman all over, and so was his family.

Mark Twain, *Huckleberry Finn,* 1884

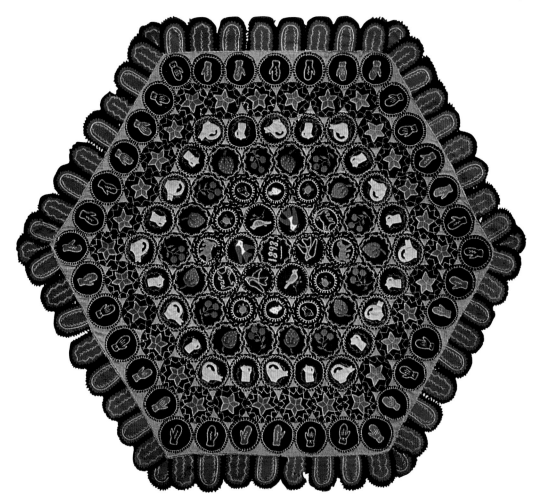

"Penny" Table Rug, artist unknown; 1893, New England. Appliquéd and embroidered wool on machine-pieced cotton backing. 42 x 47 inches (106.6 x 119.3 cm). © Shelburne Museum, Shelburne, Vermont.

In colonial America during the first half of the eighteenth century, carpets were considered much too valuable to be used on the floor. Carpets were originally used as coverings for tables and chests, while floors remained bare or covered with fine sand that was swept into patterns each day with a broom. Written references to floor rugs in the homes of the wealthy started appearing in the late 1700s, but purchased carpets remained too expensive for most Americans through a good part of the 1800s.

Economic necessity therefore inspired the women of a household to design the rugs they needed, then to sew, hook, braid, weave, and embroider them. In fact, hooked rugs were a North American invention, originating in the United States and Canada. Strips of wool fabric, not yarn, were used to

Fan Rug, Marie Sugar; 1999. Hooked rug: h. 24 in. (61 cm) w. 34 in. (86.4 com). Photo by James Ferry

The Crow, Marie Sugar; 1998. Hooked rug: h. 21 in. (53.3 cm) w. 14 in. (35.6 cm). Photo by James Ferry

form loops that made up a hooked rug. The designs usually incorporated simple, outlined shapes in muted colors, with little attention paid to realistic scale or proportion.

Many of the old rugs that survive are beautiful, and we marvel at the technical skill of their makers. Rug making is still widely practiced in America, although commercially available patterns have probably had a dampening effect on the number of original designs.

PENNY RUGS

Even after it became more common to use rugs on the floor, table rugs were still extensively used to protect furniture surfaces. Textiles of any kind were among a family's most valuable possessions, and table rugs were fine ways to put even the smallest scraps of fabric to a useful purpose. In the late 1800s, it became popular to make tabletop coverings called penny rugs, coin rugs, or dollar

Good Luck Penny Rug, Barbra Viall; 2000. Cotton, wool, cotton thread, copper burrs: h. 9½ in. (24.1 cm) w. 33½ in. (85.1 cm). Photo by artist

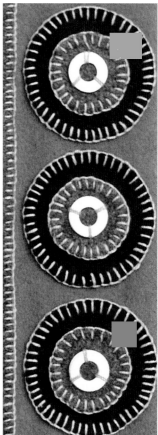

rugs, using wool that had been felted, i.e., washed until it shrank. An early American style of applique, these rugs were decorated with round fabric cutouts and simple shapes of animals or flowers. The shapes were layered, appliqued to the rug with contrasting colors of embroidery thread in a *blanket stitch* (also called *buttonhole stitch*), and sometimes embellished with other embroidery stitches. The rugs got their name from the coins used to create the circular templates.

FLOORCLOTHS

Imported English floorcloths appeared as early as 1650 in America. Made of heavy canvas decorated with paint, they featured contrasting blocks of color in tilelike designs. The patterns evolved into freer and more elaborate designs by the eighteenth century.

Multimedia Sheep Penny Rug (and detail), Barbra Viall; 1999. Wool, cotton thread, metal washers, zippers, buttons, snaps: h. 24¼ in. (61.6 cm) w. 22 in. (55.9 cm). Photo by artist

Good Luck Penny Rug (detail), Barbra Viall; 2000. Cotton, wool, cotton thread, copper burrs: h. 9½ in. (24.1 cm) w. 33½ in. (85.1 cm). Photo by artist

Hallway Floorcloth at the John Jay Homestead, Janet Flinchbaugh; 1999. Canvas, acrylic paint: l. 11.1 m. w. 6.8 m. Photo by the staff of the John Jay Homestead

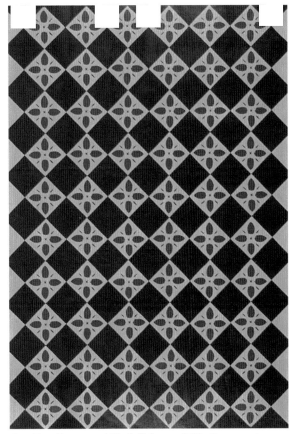

Compass Floorcloth, Dennis and Sheila Belanger; 2000. Canvas, paint: h. 72 in. (182.9 cm) w. 96 in. (243.8 cm). Reproduction of eighteenth-century floorcloth. Photo by Sierra Photo

Pine Cone, Dennis and Sheila Belanger; 2000. Canvas, paint: h. 72 in. (182.9 cm) w. 96 in. (243.8 cm). Reproduction of eighteenth-century floorcloth. Photo by Sierra Photo

American-made cloths debuted around 1750, copying 100-year-old English patterns. The cloths reached their peak from the mid-1700s to the century's end, and can be seen in paintings by early American artists such Erastus Salisbury Field and the well-known portraitist Gilbert Stuart. Two 1838 paintings by Field portray children standing on a floorcloth with a boldly stylized red, green, and ochre pattern, like the one shown in the lower right photograph.

Taverns and prosperous households used floorcloths that covered the entire floor. Made of closely woven canvas, the floorcloths were stiffened with starch and painted with bold geometric designs made durable by repeated coats of paint. A compass in a diamond field was a common New England pattern; the compass gives the pattern a maritime feel. Some historic houses and inns still display their original floorcloths.

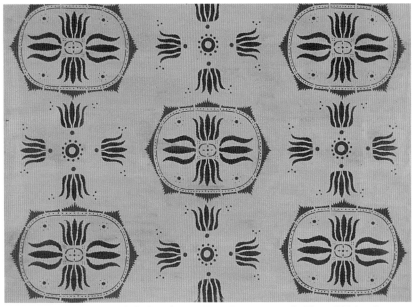

Erastus Floorcloth, Dennis and Sheila Belanger; 2000. Canvas, paint: h. 72 in. (182.9 cm) w. 96 in. (243.8 cm). Reproduction of eighteenth-century floorcloth. Photo by Sierra Photo

Tavern Pattern Floorcloth

THE PATTERNS IN THIS ATTRACTIVE FLOORCLOTH WERE INSPIRED BY A DESIGN THAT WAS COMMONLY FOUND IN COLONIAL TAVERNS. MADE OUT OF HEAVY CANVAS AND PAINTED WITH A STENCIL, THE FLOORCLOTH IS EXTREMELY DURABLE, EASY TO CLEAN, AND HOLDS UP WELL IN HEAVY-TRAFFIC AREAS.

DENNIS BELANGER,
Designer

MATERIALS

– 1 yard (0.9 m) of #10 cotton canvas, primed and stretched*
– Acrylic latex ceiling paint in flat white
– Acrylic latex paint in yellow ocher, brick red, and green
    *Available from marine suppliers or arts and crafts retailers

TOOLS AND SUPPLIES

– Large piece of plywood or a cement floor to serve as work surface
– Carpenter's square
– Duct tape
– Paintbrush, 3 inches (7.6 cm) wide
– Heavy shears
– Pencil
– Yardstick
– Acrylic latex contact cement or hot glue gun
– Rolling pin
– Heavy books or clothespins
– 2 foam brushes, 3 inches (7.6 cm) wide
– 2 stencil patterns on page 140
– White paper
– Sheet of polyester film
– Fine-tip permanent marker or pen
– Craft knife
– Painter's tape
– Stencil brush
– Oil-based polyurethane
– Liquid latex rubber backing (optional)

INSTRUCTIONS

1. Use the duct tape to tape the canvas to the plywood or cement floor, making sure the canvas is taut and anchoring the tape around all the edges.

2. Brush a coat of the white ceiling paint on the canvas. Wait three to four hours, then turn over the canvas and do the same to the other side. Let dry 24 hours.

3. Now you'll hem the canvas so the edges won't curl. Lay the canvas on the floor or a large table. Use the carpenter's square to make sure the floorcloth's sides and corners square up, so the edges can be mitered later.

4. Use the pencil and yardstick to draw a line 1 inch (2.5 cm) from the edges of the canvas, creating a 1-inch (2.5 cm) border on all four sides.

5. Apply the acrylic latex contact cement or hot glue gun to one edge at a time (see fig. 1), folding the edge over 1 inch (2.5 cm) and pressing down with the rolling pin. Weight the edges down with the books, or use the clothespins to hold down the edges until they're dry.

Figure 1

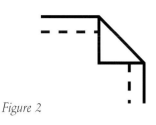

Figure 2

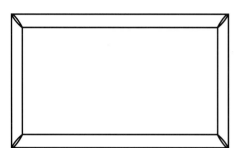

Figure 3

6. Miter the corners as shown in figure 2 and 3, applying the cement at each corner and folding it in from the point where the two 1-inch (2.5 cm) margin lines intersect. Apply more cement along each edge, and fold it in again to create a finished edge to the canvas with no raw edges showing. Secure with the books or clothespins, and let dry overnight.

7. Use a foam brush to cover the "right" side of the floorcloth with the yellow ocher paint. Let dry. Apply a second coat, and let dry overnight.

8. Use a photocopier to enlarge the two patterns on page 140. Place the sheet of polyester film on top of the traced pattern, and use the permanent marker or pen to trace the pattern onto the film. Place the film on the plywood or another hard cutting surface, and use the craft knife to cut out the pattern.

9. Put the floorcloth on a table and use the yardstick and pencil to mark off 2 inches (5.1 cm) on all four sides. Use a foam brush to paint the border freehand, or mark it off with the painter's tape and then paint. Let dry.

10. Place the oval and rectangular stencils on the floorcloth, spacing them as indicated in figure 4. Tape down the stencils with the painter's tape, then use the stencil brush to paint in the red and green colors, one color at time. When you finish stenciling in the patterns, reverse the patterns, position them on the other end (after completely wiping off any paint), and stencil them onto the floorcloth. You should now have four patterns on the floorcloth. Let dry overnight.

11. Use a foam brush to apply a coat of polyurethane over the painted surface and let dry. Following the manufacturer's instructions on drying time between coats, apply at least three more coats, and more if you wish. You may also use a foam brush to apply the liquid latex rubber backing to the underside of the floorcloth, if desired. Let dry.

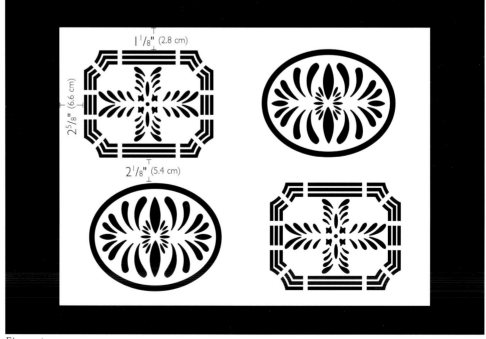

Figure 4

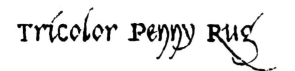

Tricolor Penny Rug

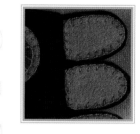

Linda L. Kerlin,
Designer

This delightful little table rug is made from simple shapes cut from felted wool that are attached with an easy blanket stitch. When you make this rug, you'll be following in the footsteps of thrifty pioneers who turned even the smallest scraps of fabric into attractive home decorations.

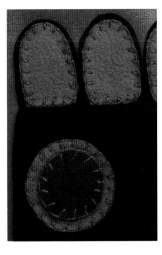

Materials and Tools

– Felted wool in the following colors and sizes*:
  – greyish blue, 13½ x 7 inches (34.3 x 17.8 cm) for the large circles and 16½ x 3½ inches (41.9 x 8.9 cm) for the medium tongues
  – gray, 10 x 5½ inches (25.4 x 14 cm) for the medium circles ("pennies")
  – black, 19 x 4 inches (48.3 x 10.2 cm) for the large tongues
  – black, two 18 x 9-inch (45.7 x 22.9 cm) pieces for the design background and rug underside
– Patterns on page 141
– Pencil (optional)
– White paper (optional)
– Sewing scissors
– Embroidery thread in metallic copper
– Embroidery needle
– Black sewing thread
  *Note: The sizes shown are for felted wool. You can either purchase felted wool, or felt it yourself as explained in step 1. If you felt your own wool, felt it before cutting it to the dimensions specified, because it will shrink.

Instructions

1. If you wish to felt your own wool, you'll need to treat it with moisture, heat, and pressure. Put the wool in very hot water with a little detergent added, and agitate it for 18 to 25 minutes. Rinse it in hot water, and dry it in a dryer.

2. Use a photocopier to enlarge the large and medium pennies and the tongue patterns on page 141, then cut them out. Place the paper patterns on the felt of the appropriate color, and cut them out. Set aside.

3. Center each medium, gray penny on top of a large, blue penny. Stitch them together with the thread and needle using a blanket stitch, also known as the buttonhole stitch (see fig. 1). Complete all eight sets.

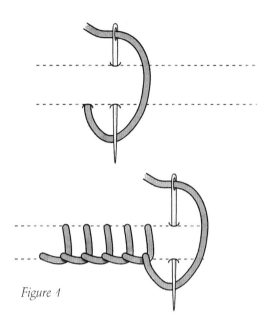

Figure 1

4. Refer to figure 2. Place the penny "stacks" on top of the 18 x 9-inch (45.7 x 22.9 cm) black background piece, and attach with a blanket stitch.

5. Lay the medium, blue tongues on top of the large black tongues, allowing about a ¼-inch (6 mm) margin of black to show. Stitch them together using a blanket stitch.

6. Referring again to figure 2, use the needle and plain black thread to attach four tongue stacks to each end of the black background piece. Use a simple stitch to tack them on.

7. Lay the decorated background on top of the underside piece, and stitch around all four sides using the black thread in a blanket stitch to connect the two pieces.

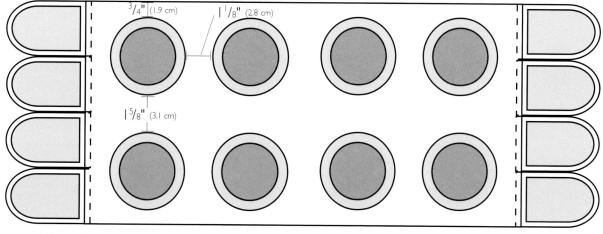

$^3/_4$" (1.9 cm) $1^1/_8$" (2.8 cm)

$1^5/_8$" (3.1 cm)

Figure 2

Quilting

The day was cold and raw. There was some snow on the ground, but not enough to warrant the use of sleighs. It was "neither sled-din' nor wheelin'." The old people sat on a board laid across the box, and had an old quilt or two drawn up over their knees.

Hamlin Garland, "Mrs. Ripley's Trip," from *Main-Travelled Roads,* 1891

No object in the history of American folk art expresses utility and comfort as eloquently as the quilt. Working patiently alone, or with family or friends, an American quilter sought to create literal and figurative comfort. A quilt would top the most important piece of furniture in a home: the bed, where so many lives were conceived, birthed, and ended.

A quilter stitches together a three-layer construction of backing material, an insulating filler material, and a top. The backing can be of any fabric. Before the invention of synthetic fibers, filler ranged from dried leaves to rags to cotton stuffing. The top is the quilter's opportunity to express artistry through creative selections of material, color, and design.

Ancient quilt remnants have been found in the Far East, the Middle East, and Europe, so it is clear that America's colonists brought quilting with them from their home countries. American quilters are responsible, however, for perfecting piece quilting in block form as a significant art form. Americans also introduced a communal aspect of the art, by starting group quilting or quilting "bees."

There are three basic types of quilt construction. *Plain* (also called *whole cloth*), *pieced*, and *appliquéd*. The terms define the primary method by which the tops are made. Whole cloth quilts are topped with one type of fabric that is sewn on in large pieces, and often feature intricately stitched patterns, such as flowers or geometric shapes, as shown in the photograph to the right. Pieced quilts have tops made up of many small pieces of fabric, either stitched or tied in place with thread, using small individual knots. Appliquéd quilts feature tops with pieces of fabric carefully positioned with edges turned in and sewn in place on a quilt top. The technique is used to create formal, often representational designs through carefully repeated motifs.

Whole cloth quilts have been found in almost every culture where people needed insulation from the cold, and, since the seventeenth century, Americans made pieced quilts out of necessity. Whereas handmade quilts today are frequently hung as wall decorations, early settlers used quilts on beds, in drafty corners, or to cover vegetables threatened with frost. Quilting was as crucial a skill as cooking, and once the quilts brought from their home countries wore thin, women used any and every textile in the household to make new quilts. Quilters made pieced quilts by cutting scraps into geometric shapes and carefully arranging them in blocks and unified patterns. Pieced quilts also had the virtue of being easy to repair.

Opposite page: Map Quilt, quiltmaker unidentified, possibly Virginia; dated 1886. Silk and cotton with silk embroidery: h. 78³/₄ in. (200cm) w. 82¹/₄ in. (208.9 cm). Collection of the Museum of American Folk Art, New York; gift of Dr. and Mrs. C. David McLaughlin. 1987.0101

Below: Patty's (detail), Martha Waterman. This contemporary quilt is a fine example of wholecloth quilting technique.

Earlier quilters may have used piecing techniques, but American quilters took an unprecedented step when they created specific block patterns that were passed down as standard designs. The subject matter and names of the designs of early pieced quilts reflected the day-to-day lives of early Americans. Motifs centered on nature, religion, and a self-sufficient lifestyle. Popular pieced designs from the eighteenth and nineteenth centuries included Flower Garden, Star of Bethlehem, Log Cabin, Drunkard's Path, Shoofly, and Tumbling Blocks. Photographs to the left are examples of traditional pieced designs.

Appliquéd quilts became popular in the mid-nineteenth century, when quilters' lives became relatively less demanding. New domestic technologies cut down on the daily hours required for food preparation and cleaning, granting upperclass women more leisure time to pursue handcrafts. America's cotton industry flourished between 1820 and 1880. This was another boon for quilters because not only did textile mills offer blankets as substitutes for time-consuming quilts, but for the first time an enormous variety of fabrics were available for specialty use on quilts. Types of preprinted fabric included calicos, florals, and chintz, which earlier could only be imported from India and, later, England. Aside from isolated poor communities in which quilts continued to be made out of necessity, quilting became a leisure pastime and a means of displaying talent. Quilting competitions became popular, and appliqué work was an opportunity to create innovative, prize-winning designs.

These "new" appliquéd quilts of the mid-1800s featured a repeated motif, or were constructed in blocks with borders above and around a scene depicted at the quilt's center. Popular appliquéd designs included

Tree of Life and scenes from the Bible. Vines and flowers were commonly depicted on borders, as shown in the photograph to the right. Appliquéd quilts were made to commemorate special family and community occasions, such as weddings, births, and christenings.

Around this time, American quilters invented quilting bees. Bees were group quilting sessions that doubled as social events for entire families and communities, similar to barn raisings. Women would do most of the sewing, usually working with cut pieces provided by the individual who would keep the quilt. Bees were also a chance for a community to pool its talent and design a quilt as a gift to honor new residents or relocating neighbors. Album quilts, made of appliquéd panels created by several quilters, became popular in the mid-1800s, at the height of quilting bees.

By the late Victorian Age, pieced quilts regained popularity, but they had a new look. Quilters sewed together pieces of fine silks with fancy embroidery stitches, creating the "crazy" quilt look (shown on page 64). Crazy quilts were often just for show. They were made smaller than a bedcover, and were used as decorative throws in parlors. At the same time, African-American women and members of Amish communities throughout America began making pieced quilts.

The Amish are a Christian religious group descended from German Anabaptists who emigrated to America in the seventeenth century. They eschew the modern world and modern technology and abhor vanity, refusing to use electricity, automobiles, or even buttons. When they took up piece quilting around the beginning of the twentieth century, Amish quilters followed self-imposed

rules about color, patterns, and the shape of cut pieces. They shunned anything bright and fancy, and stuck to a few basic designs, including geometric patterns of diamonds, patches in groups of four or nine squares, bars, or "sunshine and shadow." They also cut pieces only in squares, triangles, or rectangles. These restrictions spurred creativity and established a highly recognizable Amish quilting style shown on page 68.

African-American quilters also developed unique styles of pieced and appliquéd quilting, but expressions of individual style were

Above: Cross River Album Quilt, Mrs. Eldad Miller (1805-1874) and others, Cross River, New York; dated November 1, 1861. Cotton and silk with wool embroidery: h. 90 in. (228.6 cm) w. 75 in. (190.5 cm). Collection of the Museum of American Folk Art, New York; gift of Dr. Stanly and Jacqueline Schneider. 1980.37.54

Opposite page, top: Sunburst Quilt, possibly Rebecca Scattergood Savery (1770-1855), Philadelphia, Pennsylvania; 1835-45. Cotton: h. 118½ in. (301 cm) w. 125⅛ in. (317.8 cm). Collection of the Museum of American Folk Art, New York; gift of Marie D. and Charles A. T. O'Neill. 1979.26.02

Opposite page, below:Wildflowers Among the Cabins, Janice Maddox; 1998. Cotton fabric: h. 11½ in. (29.2 cm) w. 11½ in. (29.2 cm). Photo by Tim Barnwell

limited until slavery was abolished. Early African-Americans made quilts out of necessity, but only after emancipation could they devote more time to quilt-making for individual purposes. African-American quilts are highly recognizable because, unlike Amish quilts, they don't follow strict rules of color choice or geometry. The quilts are reminiscent of African textiles, with their bright colors, random patterns, and improvised pictorial representations of humans, animals, and plants. Also, the quilts tend to have their top pieces tied on rather than sewn.

The AIDS Quilt is possibly America's best-known contemporary quilt. Envisioned in 1985 as a symbol of healing and comfort for victims of Acquired Immune Deficiency Syndrome, the quilt features panels commemorating people who died from the disease. The original quilt displayed 1,920 panels measuring 6 x 3 foot (2 x 1 m). The panels include names and portraits of victims, and sometimes incorporate personal items, such as clothes or toys. By the year 2000, the quilt contained 44,000 panels memorializing more than 83,000 people from 39 countries. It weighed more than 50 tons (45 m tons) and would stretch for 50 miles (80.45 km) if the panels were laid end to end. The AIDS Quilt was nominated for a Nobel Peace Prize in 1989. It is the world's largest community art project, and has redefined the purposes and possibilities of community quilt-making.

One Patch Quilt, quiltmaker unidentified, Midwestern United States; dated 1921. Cotton and wool: h. 75½ in. (191.8 cm) w. 64 in. (162.6 cm). Collection of the Museum of American Folk Art, New York; gift of David Pottinger. 1980.37.54

Yo-Yo Quilt

MANY OF US REMEMBER SEE-
ING THIS WONDERFUL TYPE
OF QUILT ON OUR GRANNIES'
BEDS, AND NOW YOU CAN
EASILY MAKE ONE FOR YOUR-
SELF! THIS TECHNIQUE WAS
USED IN THE 1920S AND 1930S
TO TURN FABRIC SCRAPS INTO
LIGHT BED THROWS. YOU
WON'T NEED ANY LARGE
FRAMES OR HEAVY PIECES OF
FABRIC, AND THE WORK CAN
BE DONE BY HAND, A FEW YO-
YOS AT A TIME. YOU CAN
MAKE YOUR QUILT FROM
VINTAGE FABRICS LIKE THE
ONE SHOWN IN THE PHOTO-
GRAPH, OR SELECT CONTEM-
PORARY COLORS AND
PATTERNS THAT PLEASE YOU.

MATERIALS

– A selection of fabrics in closely woven, lightweight cottons that don't fray easily: each 4-inch (10.2 cm) yo-yo is made from a circle of fabric 8 inches (20.3 cm) in diameter and a smaller circle 1½ inches (3.8 cm) in diameter
– A piece of fabric for the quilt backing*
– Cotton flannelette (optional)
– Thread in various colors
– Thread to match the backing
  *The quilt shown measures 69 x 78-1/2 inches (175.3 x 199.4 cm). Adjust the dimensions if you use a different quantity of yo-yos.

TOOLS AND SUPPLIES

– Piece of cardboard
– Compass
– Pencil
– Craft knife or scissors
– Sewing scissors
– Paper
– Straight pins
– Upholstery needle

INSTRUCTIONS

1. Use the compass and pencil to draw two circles on the cardboard, one 8 inches (20.3 cm) in diameter and the other 2 inches (5.1 cm) in diameter. Cut them out with the craft knife. These will serve as templates for the yo-yos and their decorative centers.

2. Use the templates to help you cut out as many yo-yos and centers as you plan to use. Since you'll initially attach the yo-yos to each other in groups of four, the total number of yo-yos and centers should be a multiple of that number. The quilt shown uses 440 yo-yos arranged in 20 rows of 22 yo-yos each.

3. Create a narrow hem of fabric on the wrong side of the fabric of each yo-yo and center (see fig. 1). For consistent (though more time-consuming) hems, cut out circles of paper that are sized to allow the fabric to turn under. Turn the hem with the piece of paper inside, baste in place, then use the iron to press the hem. Remove the basting and paper.

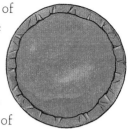

Figure 1

4. Thread a needle with the doubled thread. Leaving a long, knotted tail at the beginning, stitch a line of running stitches around the perimeter of the yo-yo (see fig. 2).

Figure 2

5. After finishing the line of stitches, place a small piece of the cotton flannelette inside the yo-yo. This will accentuate its puffy appearance, as shown in photo 1. Pull the thread tightly to gather the yo-yo (see fig. 3), making the opening as small as you can. Knot and trim the ends of the thread, and tuck them out of sight.

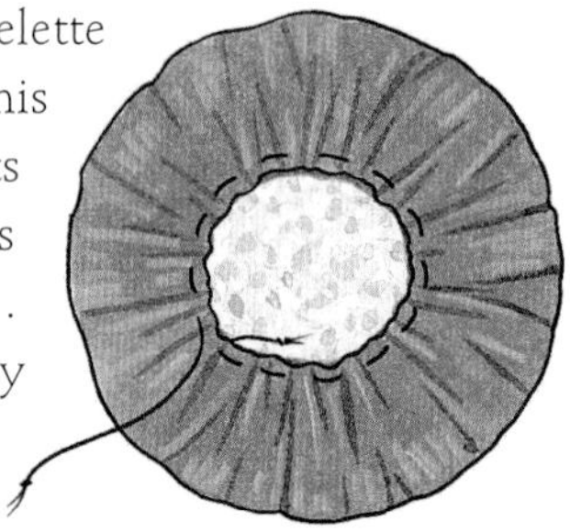

Figure 3

6. Position the gathered opening in the center of the yo-yo, and use the iron to flatten the yo-yo. Place a hemmed center in the middle on top of the gather, and stitch in place with a tiny whipstitch (see fig. 4).

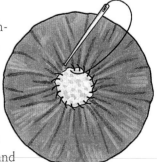

Figure 4

7. Assembling the quilt will be easier if you first join the completed yo-yos together in units of four, then join the units. Catch them on each side with four of five whipstitches, knot the threads, and cut away excess tails (see fig. 5).

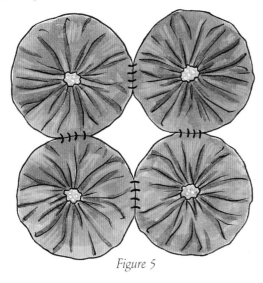

Figure 5

8. To make the fabric backing, simply turn under a ¼-inch (6 mm) margin on the raw edge, iron, and turn under another 1 or 1¼ inches (2.5 or 3.2 cm) to make a hem. Secure with the straight pins and hem with a hem-stitch, or you may choose to use a straight, ¼-inch (6 mm) stitch that will show through on the "right" side of the fabric (the hemmed

side goes on the bottom). Remove the pins and iron.

9. Now you'll attach the yo-yo assemblage to the backing with individual "ties" of thread in different colors. Lay the backing flat and put the yo-yos on top; if you position the outer rim of yo-yos so they protrude slightly over the edge of the backing, you'll create an attractive scalloped effect. Pin the yo-yos to the backing. Thread the upholstery needle with a double thread, and, starting from the yo-yo side, run it through the center of each yo-yo and back up again through the center. Tie the thread in a knot and trim it, leaving little tails about ¼ inch (6 mm) long. Change thread colors frequently.

strippy quilt

A QUILT CONJURES UP THOUGHTS OF HEARTH AND HOME. THOUGH QUILTING IS A TIME-HONORED, TRADITIONAL HANDCRAFT, A PERSON WITH SIMPLE SEWING SKILLS CAN TAKE UP THE ART. A STRIP QUILT IS ONE OF THE EASIEST TYPES TO MAKE. MAKING A UNIQUE QUILT TO COVER YOUR BED OR DECORATE YOUR WALL IS RELATIVELY EASY WITH THE HELP OF A SEWING MACHINE AND BASTING SPRAY THAT ALLOWS YOU TO TEMPORARILY ADHERE PIECES AND REPOSITION THEM IF NECESSARY. THE FINISHED SIZE OF THIS QUILT IS 62 X 88 INCHES (155 X 220 CM).

SANDRA S. ROWLAND, Designer

MATERIALS

- Pattern on page 138
- 5 yards (4.5 m) of a variety of 100 percent cotton dress-weight fabrics in a 45-inch (114.3 cm) width to create the pieced sections (boldly printed fabrics are lively and suit a strippy quilt)
- Basting spray*
- 1⅔ yards (1.4 m) of 100 percent cotton, dress-weight fabric in a 45-inch (114.3 cm) width to create the outline strips
- 1 yard (.9 m) of 100 percent cotton, dress-weight fabric in a 45-inch (114.3 cm) width to create the inner border strips
- 5¼ yards (4.7 m) of 100 percent cotton, dress-weight fabric in a 45-inch (114.3 cm) width to create the quilt backing
- Medium-loft cotton or poly/cotton blend batting, 66 x 90 inches (167.64 x 228.6 cm) minimum
- Cotton, cotton-wrapped polyester, or size .044 nylon monofilament thread to match the fabric
- 8.75 yards (7.9 m) of ½-inch (1.3 cm) double-fold binding
*Available at sewing stores

TOOLS AND SUPPLIES

- Scissors
- Sewing machine
- Iron
- Basting spray or tacks or pins (optional)
- Sewing needle (optional)

INSTRUCTIONS

1. From the 5 yards (4.5 m) of fabric, cut an assortment of strips along the fabric's length, creating random widths of 1 to 2 inches (2.5-5.1 cm). This will give you strips 42 to 45 inches (105 to 112.5 cm) long. Refer to the pattern on page 138 as needed for steps 1 through 7.

2. Sew some of the assorted strips along their lengths to create four pieced sections measuring 14¼ x 45 inches (36.2 x 112.5 cm). As shown in figure 1, sew the strips using ¼-inch (6 mm) seams in alternate directions. This will prevent the fabric from stretching out of shape. Open up the seams, and use the iron to press them flat. As you continue to make different sections of the quilt top, press any seam allowances open after you've sewn the seam.

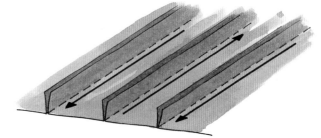

Figure 1

3. Now you'll sew more of the assorted strips together to make four sections that will serve as the outer border of the quilt. Two of the pieces will measure 9 x 72 inches inches (22.9 x 192.9 cm), and two will measure 9 x 62 inches (22.9 x 155 cm). Cut the strips into 9-inch (22.9 cm) lengths, and sew them together along their long edges, sewing the seams in alternating directions as you did in step 2.

4. Cut the 5¼-yard (4.7 m) piece of fabric crossways into two pieces. With right sides together, pin the pieces together along one

long edge, then sew them togather. Remove the pins, and cut away any extra length so the piece is 88 inches (220 cm) long. This piece will serve as the quilt backing.

5. Cut three strips measuring 4½ x 45 inch (11.4 x 112.5 cm) from the 1⅔ yards (1.4 m) of fabric. Arrange the large whole-piece "outline" strips between the four sections of fabric strips, as shown in the pattern. Using a ¼-inch (6 mm) seam, sew the outline strips to the pieced sections.

6. Cut six strips measuring 2½ x 45 inches (6.4 x 112.5 cm) from the yard of fabric. These will form the inner border strips, as shown in the pattern. Sew the inner border strips to the top and bottom, and use the iron to press the inner, raw edge of the attached strip to form a clean edge (you'll lap the end of the side border under it a bit later). Sew two strips together to make one side border, and repeat to make the other side border. Sew the side borders to the section you've already assembled, lapping the ends of the side borders under the ends of the top and bottom borders. Sew the border ends together.

7. Pin the 9-inch- (22.9 cm) wide outer border sections to the assembly, and sew them together. Remove the pins. You've now made the quilt top!

8. Layer the quilt top, the batting, and the backing, as shown in figure 2.

9. Use the basting spray or basting tacks or pins to baste the layers of the quilt top, batting, and backing in place, or use the needle and thread to sew them together by hand with a large basting stitch. Make sure the right side of the top faces up and the right side of the quilt backing faces down as they will appear in the finished quilt.

10. Either by hand or with a sewing machine, quilt all the layers together, being sure the needle pierces all the layers. Use either uniformly straight or consistently curved lines; the stitches will show on both sides of the quilt.

11. Remove the basting stitches, tacks, or pins. If necessary, trim the edges of the batting and backing so they've even with the quilt top.

12. Open up the double-fold binding. Sew the ends of the pieces of binding together if necessary to make a continuous 8.75 yard (7.9 m) length of binding. Pin the binding over the raw edges of the quilt. Sew the binding to the quilt, all the way around, tucking under a small margin at the end to create a clean edge and lapping it over the starting point.

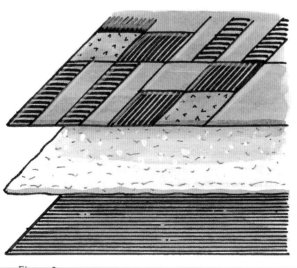

Figure 2

outsider art

So the young Dutchman spent the afternoons at his dormer window reading and glancing down at the little casement opposite, where a small, rude shelf had lately been put out, holding a row of cigar-boxes with wretched little botanical specimens in them trying to die.

George Washington Cable, *Old Creole Days,* 1879

Outsider art owes its name to its makers' origins, and it was not identified by critics and collectors as an important category of American folk art until the twentieth century. Today the term is almost a misnomer, given that the work of outsider artists is eagerly collected and shown in mainstream museums. Tramp art, prisoner art, recycled art, and memory-ware are all recognized genres of outsider art.

Historically, outsider artists are self-taught, and they belong to cultural groups in America that have been politically and economically disenfranchised, including women, the poor, Hispanics, and African-Americans (especially in the Deep South). Their subject matter includes intensely personal, sometimes eccentric, statements or political messages. Without formal art training, outsider artists work independently of aesthetic or technical standards imposed by mainstream thinking. Using painting, sculpture, collage, drawing, fiber art, found objects, or any combination thereof, the artists are free to pursue their own visions with strikingly original results. Outsider art includes utilitarian objects that have been given additional, decorative elements by the artist, but it also can exist strictly for its own sake as the expression of a creative vision, not a utilitarian purpose.

Barometer Case, Michael Cornish; Found objects.
Courtesy of the John & Linda Sholl Collection

Tramp art, also called *chipwork*, is probably the most easily-recognized but most misattributed form of American outsider art, because its makers weren't exclusively tramps. Such a large body of tramp art exists, and the hobby of chip carving appears so often in written history, that it's likely that itinerant laborers and the gainfully employed in the lower and middle classes pursued chipwork as a hobby.

Tramps may have been mistakenly credited for chipcarving because chipwork is often made from free materials, such as discarded cigar boxes and packing crates. Cigar boxes were plentiful for two reasons: cigars were status symbols beginning in the late nineteenth century, and by law the boxes could not be re-used. The thin, soft wood was easily carved with a pocket knife, and glue or tiny nails were enough to secure pieces.

Frame, artist unknown; date unknown. Courtesy of the John & Linda Sholl Collection

The history of chipcarving is one case in which the myth of hardscrabble American ingenuity is greatly exaggerated. Wooden objects decorated with chip carving have been found in Europe since medieval times, and the carving and decorating techniques were brought to America by German and Scandinavian immigrants, many of whom probably apprenticed as wood carvers. The painstaking, time-consuming art form flourished from Civil War days through the 1930s. Soldiers practiced carving, making gifts for loved ones and goods for barter. Similarities among historic examples of tramp art suggest that printed instructions were disseminated, but no surviving texts have been discovered.

Dresser or Washstand, Erastus Hanor; 1910. Cigar box wood. Courtesy of the John & Linda Sholl Collection

Layering and notch-carving are the decorative techniques characteristic of tramp art. Objects are crafted from layers of wood that are always constructed in geometric, heart, or pyramid shapes built up like a ziggurat, with the layers getting smaller as they get higher. Variations of layering include an interlocking layering method called the Crown of Thorns. The artist carves a pattern of V-shaped notches along each layer's edges before adding it to the piece and matching the notches. In addition to a pocketknife, a veining tool (also called a u-curved gouging chisel) and a flat chisel are useful tools.

Hearts, leaves, religious images, and flowers were common, as were patriotic symbols of flags, stars, and eagles, and the colors red, white, and blue. Finishes and embellishments are eclectic, including paint, lacquer, stain, pull knobs, mosaic, photos, or parts of the original box label.

Tramp art's popularity declined when its free materials disappeared, and mass media entertainment began displacing hand craft as a means of filling Americans' leisure time. Cigarettes, sold in small paper packs, were marketed as a cheap, fashionable alternative to cigars, and cardboard packaging edged out wood.

Recycled art should not be confused with tramp art. Recycled art is a reflection of America's material overabundance. The poor, frugal, or clever collect disposable objects for artistic use, including bottle caps, matchsticks, frozen-dessert sticks, buttons, pencils, dish shards, window panes, glass containers, or food labels. Some recycled art makes a statement about our "disposable" society, but for many artists, the material is simply a material.

Prison art is the name given to objects made by inmates from materials they scavenged in their day-to-day lives behind bars, including objects woven from cigarette packs, gum wrappers, and paper bags. Art created from simple materials by prisoners dates back to the American Civil War. Art therapy programs were introduced to correctional facilities in the 1960s as a rehabilitative tool, but safety restrictions continue to limit the availability of materials. Soap is carved with dull instruments, and paper is still a mainstay material, but such restrictions continue to inspire the historic ingenuity at the heart of prison art.

Top left: Ditty or Jewelry Box, Dick Lenard Baker (1877-1960). Decoupaged with postal stamps. Courtesy of the John & Linda Sholl Collection

Top right: Prison Art, artists unknown; c. 1930. Woven cigarette packs, dimensions various. Photo by Rick Ladd

Bottom right: Comic Book Lamp, Rick Ladd; 1989. Woven pages from comic books, h. 20 in. (50.8 cm) w. 8 in. (20.3 cm) d. 8 in. (20.3 cm). Photo by the artist

Bottom left: Miniature furniture, artist and date unknown. Tin cans, fabric. h. 4 in. (10.2 cm) w. 2 in. (5.1 cm). These tiny chairs were constructed as doll furniture, pincushions, and whimsies. Photo by Evan Bracken.

Memoryware is another type of outsider art that describes sentimental pieces of art made from the literal pieces of one's personal or family history. In this art form, meaningful objects or fragments are permanently adhered to the surface of a container or other object. Questions about the origins of memoryware in American folk art remain unanswered, and it has been used for different purposes by different makers.

Memoryware, Terry Taylor, 1995-1996. Ceramic vases, mixed media, gold paint: dimensions various.

Memoryware is often associated with African-American funerary vessels, made to commemorate the life of the recently deceased, and placed at gravesites. These vessels are linked to the memorial practices of various ancient African tribes, in which tombs or graves are embedded with items relating to the history of the dead or the objects last used by the dead. The leaving of pebbles, glass, and fragments of objects at a relative's graveside is a documented tradition among early African-Americans, but there are no concrete records of memoryware found in historically African-American cemeteries.

It has been documented that Americans of European descent made memoryware to mourn a deceased loved one, keeping it in the house. Some surviving nineteenth-century memoryware also appears to have been made with a frivolous intent. Lighter examples of memoryware date from the Victorian Era, when American women of European descent gathered beloved clutter and stuck it on pots, jugs, jars, and other common objects. Materials included sewing notions, bits of family heirloom china or found shards, jewelry, seashells, bark, nuts, pods, mirrors, beads, toys, coins, sentimental keepsakes from children or spouses, and keys. Objects were affixed with putty, cement, or plaster.

Shard art, or *pique assiette*, is an art form similar to memoryware and derives its name from Raymond Eduard Isidore of France. Starting in the 1930s, Isidore compulsively decorated every surface of his home and its contents with bits of pottery and glass shards. His neighbors called him picassiette, a derogatory term translating into "stealer of plates." The photo below is an example of shard art.

Tea and Company, Michele Petno, 1999. Pique-assiette over silver teapot, mixed media: dimensions various.

Twisted Tin Can Furniture Trio

MATERIALS

- Diagrams on page 137
- Clean, empty cans, at least two of the same type and size for each chair*
- Metal primer (optional)
- Enamel paint in the colors of your choice (optional)
- Fabric scraps
- Cotton or quilt batting
- Cardboard

  *You'll use one can as a template, and the other(s) as raw material. You can make the furniture from cans of different sizes. Simply adapt the patterns on page 137 by adjusting the number of strips you cut, removing any excess strips or adding more.

TOOLS AND SUPPLIES

- Safety can opener, the kind with handles that can open to 180°
- Heavy work gloves
- Tin snips
- Metal ruler
- Awl or other scribing tool
- Masking tape
- Needle-nose pliers
- Sardine can key
- Small level
- White glue
- Small paintbrush
- Craft knife
- Scissors

THE ART OF MAKING MINIATURE WHIMSIES FROM TIN CANS IS A RARE AMERICAN FOLK CRAFT. YOU CAN EASILY CUT TIN CANS INTO THIN STRIPS AND CURL THEM TO CREATE EXQUISITE, DOLL-SIZED FURNITURE WITH THE LOOK OF VICTORIAN WICKER. WHETHER YOU CHOOSE TO PAINT THEM, OR LEAVE THEM UNPAINTED TO HINT AT THEIR TRUE ORIGINS, IS UP TO YOU! THE EDGES OF CUT TIN ARE VERY SHARP, SO ALWAYS WEAR WORK GLOVES AND BE CAREFUL WHEN YOU HANDLE THE MATERIAL.

INSTRUCTIONS

1. First, you'll make a template from a can to guide you in marking the width of strips to be cut in the other cans. Use the safety can opener to remove the top and bottom lids from a can of the same type and size you'll use to make the furniture. Put on the work gloves and use the tin snips to remove the rims and side seam. Around the top and bottom of the can, use the ruler and awl to mark slits spaced ⅛ inch (3 mm) apart, and ¼ inch (6 mm) deep. Adjust the measurements if necessary to conform to the circumference of the can you've chosen.

2. Use the can opener to remove the lids of the can(s) to be used for the doll furniture, and cut the rims off with the tin snips. Use the snips to remove the side seams by cutting down both sides of the seam.

3. Position the template over the can so its edge is even with the seam line, and use the masking tape to fix it in place.

4. Use the awl to scribe a mark at each slit in the template along the top and bottom ends of the can, leaving marks on the can. Remove the template.

5. Use the ruler and awl to draw lines connecting the matching top and bottom marks on the can.

6. Use the tin snips to cut along each line down to the bottom rim of the can, creating strips of equal width around the entire can (see fig. 1).

7. Make a curling tool from the sardine can key by using the tin snips to cut off the end, leaving a small prong at the end.

8. Follow the diagram on page 137 for the chair you're making, using the needle-nose pliers and curling tool to bend the strips up or down, to twist them, and to create curls (see fig. 2).

9. Create individual connectors to use as required by cutting narrow, ½-inch-long (1.3 cm) strips from an extra can. As shown in the diagrams, bend the connectors in place around groups of strips to secure them.

10. As shown in figure 2, use the curling tool to create the curls on the ends of strips by inserting the end of each strip in the prongs of the tool, curling the strip, then removing the tool. If the diagram calls for extra curlicues, cut 4-inch-long (10.2 cm) strips from an extra can, attach them with the connectors, and curl them.

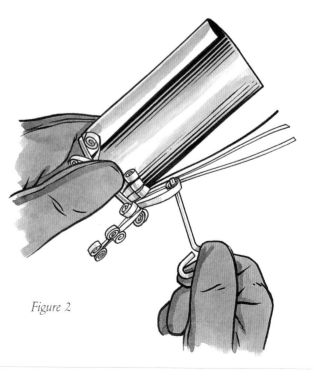

Figure 2

Figure 1

11. Use the level to check how level the completed chair is. Even out the legs if necessary by bending them with the curling tool.

12. If you don't want to leave the chair *au naturel*, use the brush to apply the metal primer to the chair, and let dry. Paint with the enamel color of your choice, applying at least two coats.

13. To add an upholstered seat or back to your chair, use the craft knife to cut the cardboard to the shape of the seat or back. Lay the cardboard pattern on the fabric and cut it out with the scissors, adding a 1-inch margin. Remove the cardboard.

14. Put the batting in the middle of the cardboard, then place the fabric on top. Wrap the fabric under the edges of the cardboard and use the white glue to glue the fabric in place. Let dry.

15. Put the cushion in the chair, gluing it to the strip designed to hold the chair back, if that is part of your design.

Folded Paper Bullseye Mirror Frame

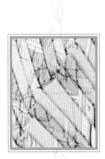

OLD WORLD MAPS WERE USED TO MAKE THIS ELEGANT MIRROR FRAME, BUT ANY KIND OF PAPER OR FOIL CAN WORK. WORLD MAPS HAVE LOTS OF BLUE, AND ROAD MAPS CONTAIN INTERESTING GRAPHICS. SIMPLY KEEP FOLDING THE SEGMENTS AND FITTING THEM INSIDE EACH OTHER UNTIL YOU HAVE A CONTINUOUS PIECE AS BIG AS YOU NEED. SELECT A SMALL MIRROR FOR YOUR FIRST PROJECT WHILE YOU'RE MASTERING FOLDED PAPER TECHNIQUE.

RICK LADD,
Designer

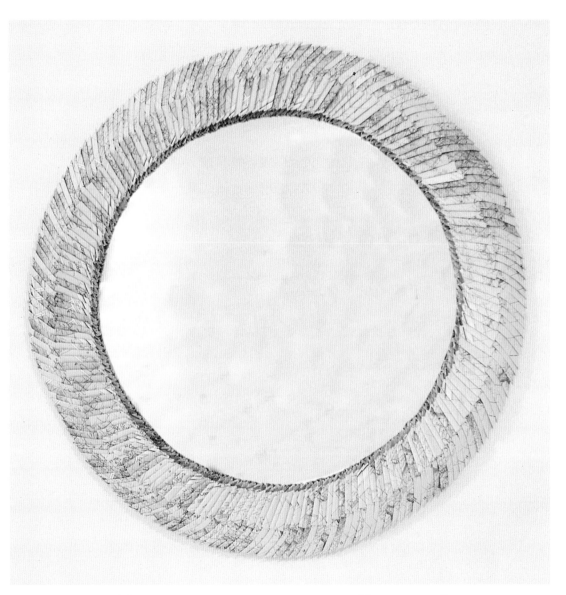

MATERIALS

– Bullseye mirror*
– Old road maps
  *The mirror shown has a 32-inch (81.3 cm) circumference, and the frame required 30 wall-sized maps deconstructed into 6 x 12-inch (15.2 x 30.5 cm) pieces.

TOOLS AND SUPPLIES

– Craft knife or scissors
– Silicone adhesive
– Caulk gun
– Piece of paper in a size that will cover the mirror glass
– Masking tape
– Clear spray-on acrylic sealer

INSTRUCTIONS

1. Use the craft knife or scissors to separate the road maps into 3 x 6-inch (7.6 x 15.2 cm) sections. The larger the pieces of paper are, the bigger your frame will be.

2. Fold a section in half crossways, making a 3 x 3-inch (7.6 x 7.6 cm) square (fig. 1). Be sure the printed map is showing on both sides of the square.

3. Fold in half again, then again (fig. 2).

4. Fold the top corners in and down to the midpoint of the square, making a shape with a silhouette that looks like a little house with a peaked roof (fig. 3).

5. Using a vertical fold, fold the "house" in half (fig. 4).

6. Now, you'll pinch the bottom and bring it up so the tab tails face up at the same time that you force them halfway into the folded top (figs. 5 and 6).

7. Fit each segment inside the previous segment, by folding the tab of the previous section over and inside the segment you're adding. Keep all of the tabs facing in.

8. Once you've completed enough segments to make the circle that forms the frame, connect the circle by folding the first and last segments together.

9. Use the caulk gun to apply a bead of silicone adhesive to the edge of the mirror. Standing above the mirror, press the folded paper in place, being careful to lay it in as perfect a circle as possible. Let dry.

10. Cover the mirror glass with the taped-down piece of paper, taking care to cover the

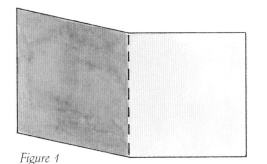

Figure 1

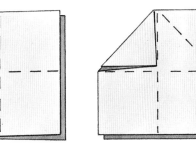

Figure 2   *Figure 3*

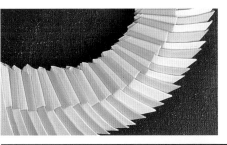

Figure 5   *Figure 6*

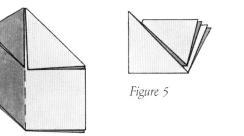

Figure 4

edges. Spray the frame with the clear acrylic sealer and let dry. Remove the paper and tape.

Tramp Art Picture Frame

Don't be surprised if you find this tramp art object irresistible: it exudes character and simple elegance. The number of layers of wood used in this project determine its complexity and overall effect. You can simplify the frame by making it with only one layer of wood atop the basic construction.

Daniel Strawser, Jr.,
Designer

MATERIALS

– Wooden picture frame
– Cigar boxes (found at tobacco shops and garage and yard sales)
– Acrylic paints

TOOLS AND SUPPLIES

– Pencil
– Paper
– Straight edge
– Tape measure
– Compass, pill bottle, or cup (optional)
– Scissors
– Coping saw or scroll saw
– Razor knife or small triangular file
– Wood glue
– Hammer
– $1/2$-inch (1.3 cm) 20 gauge brads
– Drop cloths
– Small paintbrush
– Aerosol acrylic-based varnish

INSTRUCTIONS

1. Remove the glass from your frame, if necessary.

2. Using the pencil, paper, straight edge, and tape measure, make one sketch for each layer you plan to add to each of the four sides of your frame. These sketches will be templates you use when cutting pieces of cigar box. The layers should decrease in dimension relative to the thickness of the material. For example, if you are using $3/16$-inch-(4.8 mm) thick wood layer atop a piece measuring 1 x $6\ 1/2$ inches (2.54 x 16.5 cm), then the layer should measure $5/8$ x $6\ 1/8$ inches (1.6 x 15.5 cm). (Note that the $3/16$ inch measurement is subtracted from each side.) If you plan to mount round wood pieces as accents on the corners of your frame, as shown in the project photo, trace a circle onto the paper using a compass, the cap or bottom of the pill bot-

tle, or the cup (of whatever size fits your design).

3. After using the saw to cut the pieces of cigar box, use the razor knife or file to notch the pieces of cigar box you plan to layer atop your frame base. There are two ways to make the notches. Figure 1 shows the wood is notched in from the edge. You can create notches by using the razor knife to make two angled cuts toward each other (see fig. 2). Sometimes making a straight cut into the depth of the notch can prevent splitting on either side. Notching can also be done with the small triangular file; push the file down and outward from the center of the area to be notched. For optimum visual effect, lightly pencil a guideline equal to the thickness of the material. By notching along these guidelines, you will create notches as wide as the wood is thick.

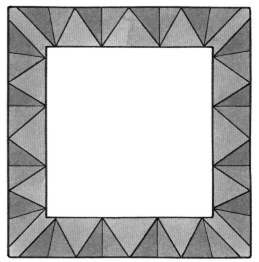

Figure 1

4. When you have notched all the layers to your satisfaction, center each layer atop the frame base. Glue each layer in its place. Nail each layer down with a brad every 4 or 5 inches (5.1 to 7.6 cm). Allow the glue to dry thoroughly before handling. To avoid staining your work area, lay out drop cloths, then use the small paintbrush to apply the acrylic paints. Let dry. You may also spray on the varnish if desired.

Figure 2

Memory Jug

GOLD PAINT LENDS ELEGANCE TO THIS SUMPTUOUS VERSION OF AN OLD-FASHIONED MEMORY JUG. IT'S EASY TO CREATE AN INSTANT FAMILY HEIRLOOM BY USING OLD COSTUME JEWELRY AND SMALL, MEANINGFUL PIECES OF BRIC-A-BRAC TO DECORATE YOUR JUG.

TERRY TAYLOR,
Designer

MATERIALS

– Ceramic jug, crock, or vase
– Pins, earrings, bracelets, necklaces, charms, or other costume jewelry
– Small objects such dice, game pieces, toys, or artificial flowers
– Acrylic modeling paste
– Gesso or base-coat paint
– Gold metallic paint*
– Antiquing glaze (optional)
  * Acrylic paints are acceptable, but oil-based metallic paints have more sheen.

TOOLS AND SUPPLIES

– Diagonal wire cutters
– Flat file
– Wax paper
– Small palette knife or disposable knife
– Flat-nosed jewelry pliers
– Masking tape
– Two small paintbrushes
– Rag

INSTRUCTIONS

1. Use the diagonal wire cutters to remove all pin backs, posts, and findings from the jewelry. With the flat file, file off any protruding parts from the jewelry backs and small objects.

2. Place your vessel upright on a length of wax paper. The wax paper will protect your work surface, and keeping the vessel upright as you work will help you gauge the effect of the decorations.

3. Spread a generous amount of the acrylic modeling paste about $1/16$ inch (.25 cm) thick and three inches (7.6 cm) wide around the base of the vessel (not its actual bottom).

4. Use the palette knife to spread a generous amount of the modeling paste on the back of a piece of jewelry. Fix it to the modeling-paste-covered base; you don't need to press the jewelry flat against the vessel, but it should be secure. Work around the base of the vessel, spreading paste and adding more jewelry or other small objects. Let the base area dry for 24 hours.

5. When dry, the base area provides support for additional pieces. Work around the vessel, adding paste and placing additional objects. Again, cover no more than an area 3 inches (7.6 cm) wide, or the objects will fall off. Let the area dry at least for eight hours before continuing.

6. If you add objects that aren't flat, after you fix them with the paste, secure them to the surface with a length of the masking tape. This gives them additional support while they dry.

7. When the vessel is completely covered, and it has dried for at least 24 hours, use a

paintbrush to coat the surface with the gesso or base-coat paint. Use a dabbing motion to get paint into the nooks and crannies to completely cover the surface. Let dry.

7. Paint the vessel with at least two coats of the metallic paint, using dabbing motions to achieve complete coverage. It's helpful to turn the vessel upside down to check if there are any uncovered areas. Let dry.

8. If desired, brush the antiquing glaze on the vessel, and use the rag to gently wipe away any excess. Let dry.

Rustic craft with trees, twigs, and bark

Tom....picked up and inspected several large semi-cylinders of the thin white bark of a sycamore, and finally chose two which seemed to suit him. Then he knelt by the fire and painfully wrote something upon each....[O]ne he rolled up and put in his jacket pocket, and the other he put in Joe's hat and removed it to a little distance from the owner.

Mark Twain, *Adventures of Tom Sawyer,* 1876

Bench sideboard, Ernest Stowe, c. 1910-1911, Upper Saranac Lake, NY

Rustic furniture and objects made with tree limbs, twigs, roots, burl, and bark in their natural states were products of a "folk" craft that actually arose as a response to the tastes of wealthy aristocrats and industrial plutocrats with money to spend. In the mid-nineteenth century, American landscape designer Andrew Jackson Downing introduced ideas from the "back to nature" movement, then in full swing in Europe and England. The movement was a reaction against classically ordered gardens and Victorian formality, and Downing was its American proponent, advocating rustic furnishings in outdoor settings. Calvert Vaux and Frederick Law Olmstead, who created great public parks such as Central Park in Manhattan, and Prospect Park in Brooklyn, were inspired by Downing. Wealthy industrialists, such as J. Pierpont Morgan and Alfred G. Vanderbilt, visited the parks and found their rustic elements so charming that they began creating their own rustic "camps" at their summer homes in the Adirondack Mountains of northern New York.

Americans of more modest means in the late 1800s also found the style very appealing. They escaped on vacations and to country homes in reaction to the problems of industrialization and urbanization. Rustic furniture gave them the wholesome feeling of being in touch with nature, or served as reminders of vacations.

To meet the demand, Scots-Irish living in the Appalachian Mountains in North and South Carolina and West Virginia started building and selling rustic furniture to tourists. They created a style of rustic seating in the 1870s called *bentwood furniture,* in which molds are used to bend hickory saplings or willow into curved shapes to form seat frames and arms. Wood slats are then added for seats and backs. *Root and twig furniture* also came out of the Appalachians. More rustic enterprises sprang up in rural areas desperate for more income, especially during the Depression. Hickory was tree-farmed on a massive scale in the Midwest as material for mass-produced "Old Hickory Furniture." The Amish of Indiana and Ohio sold bent-twig rockers

Arch settee, David Robinson, NY

Entrance gate, Ausable Club, NY

Bent willow chair, Greg Adams, IN

End table, cherry, Catskill Mountain driftwood, Judd Weisburg, NY

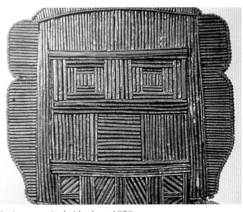

Antique mosaic chairback; c. 1920

Birch bark baskets, Ojibwa Indians, MN. Courtesy Ladyslipper Designs

and tables at flea markets and fairs, where you can still find them. Native American tribes in Maine, New York, and Florida made rustic furniture specifically for tourists, and in the Northeast, souvenir picture frames and accessories were made from balsam, pine, and birch. Adirondacks craftsmen catered to wealthy summer residents, making fantastic rustic furniture that used all parts of the tree and incorporated elements including leather, bones, horns, hooves, and even taxidermy! Ernest Stowe and Lee Fountain are the most recognized Adirondack makers, Stowe working in birch bark, and Fountain making birch rockers and tables.

or half-round branches over frames, as structural and/or decorative elements of a piece of furniture. In *bark work* (photograph to left), birch, cedar, or cherry bark is harvested in the spring. After the bark is peeled like an orange from the freshly harvested wood, it's flattened for seasoning and drying. When it's dry, the bark is steamed or soaked so the shaggy part can be torn off by hand. Once the bark has dried again, it's nailed to a wooden surface or frame. The edges are often finished with mosaic work. Bark is most often used on tables and desks, cupboards, chests, picture frames, and even clock cases. Birch bark is a particularly ver-

Birch bark corner hutch, Barry Gregson, NY

Tastes change, and by the time aluminum and plastic chairs were introduced in the 1950s, the rustic furniture business sharply declined. The style was perceived as undesirable, the furniture of poor people who made it from necessity. When the 1960s counterculture began a new back-to-the-land movement focusing on natural living and self-sufficiency, those ideas percolated into mass culture. Rustic style was restored to the realm of the affluent and the fashionable, the very market that inspired it in the first place.

Today's rustic work falls into several types of craft. *Split work, mosaic,* and *Swiss work* (shown on page 90, lower right) are different names for the same craft of nailing full

Canopy bed, Judd Weisburg, NY

Side chairs, Daniel Mack, NY; 1986

satile material, and the Ojibwa Indians of Minnesota continue to produce very fine birch bark baskets and other designs.

Stick or *sapling furniture* (seen in photograph to left) is constructed from small trees and branches joined to resemble the way they grew. This type of rustic work looks deceptively fragile, and is made with and without the bark left on. *Tree and log furniture* (page 91) is made from large limbs and trunks of proportions befitting Paul Bunyan! *Bentwood furniture* (shown on lower left) is created from long, fresh branches of willow, alder, or cottonwood nailed around a frame. *Root and burl work* (shown below) uses stumps, roots, or burls (the big bumps that appear on trees) as furniture material.

Burled bed, Mike Patrick, WY

Bent willow chair, Clifton Montieth, MI

Birch Bark canoes

Whether you craft
these canoes for play-
ing pioneer or decorat-
ing a side table, they're
easy and fun to make.
Thanks to microwave
ovens, it's easy to
steam the bark to
make it pliable.

Terry Taylor,
Designer

MATERIALS

– Sheets of birch bark*
– Canoe template on page 139
– A few 3-foot (.9 m) strands of raffia
– Scrap of thin wood, basswood, or balsa, about 1 x 4 inches (2.5 x 10.2 cm)
– Acrylic stain or paint (optional)
  *Available in craft stores. If you live where birch trees are abundant, harvest the bark only from fallen trees. Removing bark from a living tree can kill the tree.

TOOLS AND SUPPLIES

– Pencil
– White paper (optional)
– Scissors or craft knife
– Paper towels
– Microwave oven
– 1-inch (2.5 cm) lengths of toothpicks or bamboo skewers, 2 for each canoe
– Magazine or stack of folded newspapers
– Awl
– Plastic container
– Tapestry needle
– Pocket knife
– Sandpaper (optional)
– Small paintbrush (optional)

INSTRUCTIONS

1. Photocopy the pattern on page 139, and cut it out . Trace the pattern on the back side of the sheet of birch bark with a pencil. Flip over the pattern and trace around it again. You will need two pieces for each canoe.

2. Use the scissors to make a test cut on a small section of the bark. If the bark feels brittle and dry, you'll need to steam it before cutting.

3. To steam the bark, wrap it in several layers of very wet paper towels, and place it in the microwave oven. Microwave it on high

power for two minutes. Remove the wrapped bark from the microwave, and unwrap it carefully as it will be hot. If the bark doesn't feel pliable, rewrap and steam it again.

4. Use the scissors to cut out the traced bark canoe shapes.

5. Put the canoe shapes together, their inner bark facing each other. Place the canoe on the magazine, and use the awl to pierce holes through the bark, approximately $1/4$ inch (6 mm) apart, from the bow to the stern (front to back) and along the keel (bottom). If you feel the bark becoming brittle and dry as you work, wrap it and steam it briefly as in step 3.

6. Fill the plastic container with hot tap water, and soak the raffia strands in the water for 10 minutes.

7. Thread the tapestry needle with a raffia strand. Start at one end of the canoe and whipstitch the two canoe pieces together. To secure the strand, begin and end the strand with several stitches through the same hole.

8. Steam the stitched canoe as in step 3. Remove it from the microwave oven and use the 1-inch (2.5 cm) lengths of toothpicks to spread apart the canoe halves. Place the canoe in a sunny spot and let dry. When dry, remove the toothpicks; the canoe will hold its shape.

9. Photocopy the oar pattern on page 139 onto the white paper, and cut it out. Trace the pattern onto the scrap of thin wood. Use the pocket knife to roughly carve out the shape, and round the sharp edges with the knife. Sand and stain the oar if desired.

poplar bark gathering pouch

Traditional basketmakers have always used abundant materials native to their region, including the bark of trees. The form of this appealingly rustic container recalls the designs of Native American tribes, who were, of course, the first true basketmakers on the North American continent. You'll want to harvest the bark in late spring, when the sap is up in the trees, to ease removal of the bark from the wood.

Nancy A. Braski,
Designer

MATERIALS

– Live poplar tree
– Dried yucca leaves, or waxed linen thread
– Dried daylily leaves

TOOLS AND SUPPLIES

– Bow saw
– Piece of ¾-inch (1.9 cm) plywood for
  work surface (optional)
– Utility knife
– Cord or string
– Large, sharp upholstery needle
– Spring-type clothespins
– Plastic bag
– Water
– Straight pins or tacks
– Short piece of board (optional)
– Rag (optional)
– Bleach (optional)

INSTRUCTIONS

1. To harvest the bark you'll need, select a poplar tree 6 to 7 inches (15.2 to 17.8 cm) in circumference, or a branch from a larger tree. If you'd like to make a basket the same size as the one in the photograph, pick a tree that will allow you to harvest a single piece 28 inches (71.1 cm) long that's not interrupted by branches. Use the bow saw to cut down the tree. Make a straight slash with the utility knife, cutting through the bark to the wood from end to end lengthwise.

2. To remove the bark from the branch,

gently run your fingers under the edges while you cut with the knife, and lift the bark off the wood. The white underside of the bark will darken as it dries.

3. Now you'll shape the bark. Flatten it on the work surface. Referring to figure 1, use the knife to carefully incise a "football" shape in the middle. Do not, however, cut entirely through the bark!

Photo 1

4. Gently push the ends of the bark together to shape the pouch. The cut area will become the pouch base (see photo 1). If necessary, incise the base outline a little deeper but don't cut all the way through or the piece will be ruined . Tie a piece of the cord around the top of the pouch and a second piece around its middle to hold the shape. Cut the top of the container, with the intended front lower than the back, if desired.

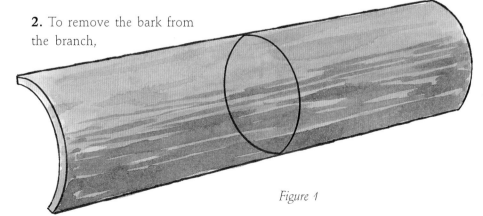

Figure 1

5. Split the dried yucca fiber into thin sewing "threads," or use the waxed linen thread. Thread the needle, knot one end, and starting at the bottom, sew the pouch edges together. Insert the needle from back to front through both pieces of bark, go up ³/₄ to 1 inch (1.9 to 2.5 cm), then insert from front to back. Sew both edges as shown in photo 2.

6. Measure the circumference of the top of the pouch. Cut a piece of thin, inner bark to match, adding 2 inches (5.1 cm). Lap the bark over the pouch lip, securing it with the clothespins. Sew it in place with a simple whipstitch using yucca or corded daylily leaves (see photo 3). To make the corded leaves, dampen the dried daylily leaves with water and put them inside the plastic bag to keep them pliable. Knot two leaves together, pin them to the work surface or board, then twist the leaves, maintaining as much tension as possible to create the cord.

Photo 2

8. Repeat step 6 to create a corded daylily handle for the pouch, but twist several leaves together to thicken the cord. Insert the ends at the top of each stitched side, and knot them on the inside of the pouch.

9. Dry the pouch by hanging it for several days in an airy room away from direct sunlight. Check the inside daily; if mold appears, remove it with a bleach-moistened rag.

Photo 3

7. To embellish the pouch, thread the needle with corded daylily, and "sew" with the cord, passing it through the holes you created when you stitched the bark over the pouch lip, but leaving a generous loop between stitches. To position a loop between every stitch, you'll need to sew around the pouch twice (see photo 4). If desired, cut long and short scraps of bark and thread them onto the loops for decoration.

Photo 4

Mosaic side table

THIS PROJECT COMES COMPLETE WITH A FIELD TRIP BECAUSE YOU'LL HAVE FUN GATHERING THE TWIGS AND BARK YOU'LL NEED TO CRAFT THIS ATTRACTIVE RUSTIC TABLE. (JUST BE SURE TO ASK PERMISSION BEFORE ENTERING PRIVATE PROPERTY!) YOU CAN ADAPT THE INSTRUCTIONS TO MAKE THE TABLE ALMOST ANY SIZE. THESE INSTRUCTIONS ARE FOR A TABLE WITH AN 18 x 18 INCH (45.7 x 45.7 CM) TOP.

TODD BARROW,
Designer

MATERIALS

– Small wooden pedestal-type table with a level, square top (or you can use a table with the legs sawn off)
– 1-inch (2.5 cm) plywood, 18 inches (45.7 cm) square
– ½-inch (1.3 cm) plywood, 14 inches (35.6 cm) square (optional)
– Five or more twisted limbs, each measuring 3 inches (7.6 cm) or more in diameter and at least as long as the table is high
– 8 lengths of saplings, each a minimum of 18 inches (45.7 cm) long and with about a 1-inch (2.5 cm) diameter
– 12 lengths of saplings, each a minimum of 13 inches (33 cm) long and with about a 1-inch (2.5 cm) diameter
– 12 lengths of saplings, each a minimum of 6 inches (15.2 cm) long and with about a 1-inch (2.5 cm) diameter
– 4 pieces of bark, each a minimum of 16 inches (40.6 cm) long and 2½ inches (6.4 cm) wide
– 4 pieces of bark, each measuring 6 x 6 x 1 inches (15.2 x 2.5 x 2.5 cm)

TOOLS AND SUPPLIES

– Pencil
– Tape measure
– Straight edge
– Hammer
– Small hand saw
– Finish nails
– Box of 10d nails
– Wood glue
– Level
– Box of 6d nails
– Craft knife or utility knife
– Hand plane, drawknife, or belt sander
– Paintbrush (optional)
– Varnish (optional)

INSTRUCTIONS

1. Use the pencil, tape measure, and straight edge to draw a square the size of your table-top on the plywood, then use the same tools to draw the pattern shown as shown in photo 1 onto the plywood.

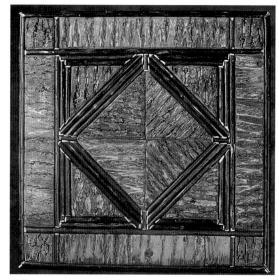

Photo 1

2. If your table doesn't have an apron underneath the top like the one shown in photo 2 on page 100, you can make one. The tabletop should overhang the apron by about 2 inches (5.1 cm). Measure and mark four strips, each 3 inches wide, on the ½-inch (1.3 cm) plywood. Two strips should be 14 inches long, or 4 inches shorter than the length of the tabletop. Make the other two strips 13 inches long to account for the thickness of the plywood. Use the saw to cut out the strips. Butt the pieces together so that the longer strips overlap the shorter ones (see fig. 1), and secure with the finish nails.

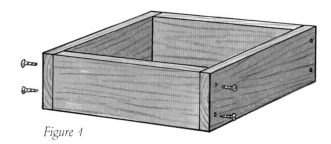

Figure 1

Lay the tabletop flat, right side down. Run a generous bead of the wood glue around the entire apron edge, then center it on the underside of the table. Let dry completely.

3. Arrange the large, twisted limbs vertically and flush against the inside of the apron as shown in the photo. You may need to use the saw to shorten limbs that are too long. Fitting one limb at a time, use the level to check that the tabletop surface is flat and even. If necessary, saw off the limb at an angle so it rests securely against the inside of the apron. Attach the legs by nailing through the apron and into each leg with two or more 10d nails.

4. Turn the tabletop right side up, and center the 18-inch-square (45.7 cm) piece of plywood on top. Nail the plywood in place using one 6d nail every 6 inches (15.2 cm). Avoid putting nails near the tabletop's edges.

5. To achieve the surface appearance shown in the photo, use the hand plane, drawknife, or belt sander to strip the bark. Remove as much of the rough outer bark as you choose, but don't make the bark less than 1/2 inch (1.3 cm) thick. Use the saw to cut your bark to fit the pattern you sketched for the tabletop design and to cover the plywood apron (as shown in photo 2).

6. Arrange the assorted saplings atop the pattern sketched on the plywood. Set aside four of the eight 18-inch lengths of 1-inch- (2.5 cm) diameter saplings; you'll use these on the outside edge of your tabletop. When necessary, use the craft or utility knife to carefully trim the edges of the saplings so they fit together without large gaps. Use smooth, vertical strokes to avoid splitting the wood.

7. Once you're ensured the pieces fit together attractively, place a thin layer of glue on the back of the saplings and the cut pieces of bark, then adhere each piece to the plywood surface by pressing the pieces in place until the glue starts to grab. This may take a minute or two. Once the pieces are firmly in place, secure the saplings with a 6d nail every 4 to 5 inches (10.2 to 12.7 cm). Don't use nails to secure the bark pieces, this could split the bark. The glue and the surrounding saplings will hold the bark in place.

8. Use the knife to trim the remaining four pieces of 1-inch-diameter (2.5 cm) sapling to fit the outside edge of the tabletop, then attach them with glue and nails.

9. If desired, use the paintbrush to apply a coat of varnish. Let dry.

Photo 2

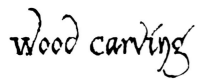

wood carving

Folk artists use what's at hand, and wood was available everywhere for early Americans to use to fashion many of the objects we know and love today, including decoys, tobacco store Indians, and crazy little whirligigs. When the weather forced farmers to stay indoors, many of them took pleasure in using a small knife to whittle useful wooden objects. Experienced craftsmen knew that hardwoods, such as walnut, oak, birch, and maple, had a firm, warp-resistant texture that was preferable for small carvings. Softer wood, such as pine or cedar, were good for larger pieces that required more carving and shaving. Function also dictated the choice of wood. A decoy body might be made of pine, for example, to resist water damage, but its head could be more easily hand-carved from softer basswood.

Black Duck, Charles E. "Shang" Wheeler (1872-1949), Stratford, Connecticut; c. 1930. Cork, wood, glass: h. 5⅞ in. (14.9 cm) w. 16 in. (40.6 cm) d. 6¾ in. (17.1 cm). Collection of the Museum of American Folk Art, New York; gift of Alastair B. Martin. 1969.01.15

WILDFOWL DECOYS

The history of decoys is inseparably inter-twined with the history of hunting in America. Native Americans made the first bird and fish decoys, designed to lure unwary animals within the reach of arrow or spear. Fish decoys made of bone have been found that date back to 2000 B.C., and in 1923, explorers in Lovelock Cave in Colorado found decoys made of reed and feathers that were immediately recognizable as the canvasback duck, still considered the most magnificent of American game ducks. The decoys were carbon-dated to A.D. 1000. Explorers and settlers in the New World observed how Indians would set stuffed game-bird skins nailed to pieces of wood out to float on waters frequented by birds. Wild birds were fooled by the decoys, and, thinking the area was safe, would fly close or land, where the Indians easily shot them.

European settlers in America adapted the Indians' methods and, around the Revolutionary War period, began carving simple wooden bird decoys. In fact, the word decoy is derived from the Dutch word for cage, *ende-kooi*. Before the Europeans started using firearms to hunt, they set out cages or traps containing live birds to attract wildfowl.

Before 1850, decoys tended to be roughly carved and rather abstract. They suggested an essential attitude or gesture that gave wild fowl who saw it from a distance the confidence to come closer to the hidden hunter's gun. Their simplicity was practical, too; fragile details or complex painting wouldn't stand up to hard wear. Some decoys were simply two-dimensional, flat cutouts that mimicked a bird's profile, but they were quite effective.

As America's population grew, the markets for wildfowl meat and feathers grew enormously. The railroads were extended and improved, and meat could be easily transported to market. The advent of the breech-loading shotgun made it easy for commercial hunters to kill birds in enormous quantities. Professional decoy makers worked in every hunting region, crafting decoys of the most common local birds. Decoys had to work well in local waters or coastal conditions, and complement hunters' methods. With competitive gunners lined up along a shoreline as a flock flew over, it quickly became apparent whose decoys were most effective.

By the mid-1800s, organized hunting emerged as a sport. Decoys became more realistic and new types appeared, including field decoys, decoys that could "fly" on wires, and "stick-ups," which are shorebird

Right: Black Bellied Plover, William D. Sarni; 2000. White pine, acrylic paint: h. 3½ in. (8.9 cm) w. 11 in. (27.9 cm) d. 3 in. (7.6 cm). Carved in the style of Russ Burr (1887-1955). Photo by artist

Ruddy Duck, William D. Sarni; 2000. Native white pine, acrylic paint: h. 5½ in. (14 cm) w. 9 in. (22.9 cm) d. 4½ in. (11.4 cm). Carved in the style of Lee Dudly (1860-1942). Photo by artist

decoys on sticks designed to be thrust into beaches or marshes.

Where demand was greatest, businessmen organized groups of carvers into cottage-industry cooperatives and began producing large quantities of decoys. The Mason Decoy Factory in Detroit, Michigan, active from 1896 to 1924, was one such cooperative. Their organization was similar to East Coast studio/factories in which wood carvers created large quantities of cigar store and circus carousel figures. Mass production of lathe-turned decoy bodies allowed carvers and painters to specialize, some in head carving, others in finishing. The studio system was eroded in the last half of the nineteenth century, however, by technical innovations, such as factory-produced rubber decoys.

Many sport hunters continued to prefer handmade wooden birds, and demand remained high for the creations of decoy makers whose work attracted the most waterfowl. Alfred Davids Laing (1811-1886) carved two-piece decoys for his own use in the tradition of New Jersey coastal decoys. Laing's work influenced the use of varied head positions in decoys (turned, tucked, and straight), and he inspired an entire generation of regional makers in Connecticut after he moved there in 1865. The decoys of Lothrop T. Holmes of Massachusetts (1824-1899) still stand as superb examples of the effective, minimalist use of paint.

Charles E. "Shang" Wheeler (1872-1949) of Connecticut carved ducks and geese of incredibly realistic size, shape, coloring, and posture, such as the exquisite black duck shown in on page 101. The duck was designed for use on exposed mud flats. Robert (1849-1915) and Catherine (d. 1953) Elliston created two-piece decoys with hollow bodies with V-shaped hulls containing lead ballasts that could ride well in swift river waters, and highly detailed, painted feathers. Virginian Nathan Cobb crafted stickup shorebirds and decoys with simple bodies and plain blocks of color, suited for use in corrosive salt water. Joseph W. Lincoln (1859-1938) of Massachusetts was famous for his geese and scoters (diving ducks also called coots).

Because of their superb painting and sculptural qualities, the decoys of A. Elmer Crowell (1862-1951) and his son Cleon in Cape Cod, of Charles and Edna Perlew in Illinois, and Lemuel and Stephen Ward in Maryland, were frequently collected as art, not for use. Their influence can be seen in the intricately detailed carving and painting used in contemporary decoys. Crowell, in fact, turned to making purely decorative decoys after 1918, after shorebird hunting was outlawed. Today, some wildfowl may still be hunted, but they cannot be sold commercially. Plastic, factory-made decoys eventually replaced wood in the mass market, but American craftsmen

Above: Black Bellied Plover, William D. Sarni; 1991. White cedar, oil paint: h. 6 in. (15.2 cm) w. 12 in. (30.5 cm) d. 3½ in. (8.9 cm). Photo by artist

Left: Ruddy Turnstone, William D. Sarni; 1996. Native white pine, acrylic paint: h. 5 in. (12.7 cm) w. 8 in. (20.3 cm) d. 2½ in. (6.4 cm). This piece is a reproduction of a decoy carved by Lothrop Holmes (1824-1899). Photo by artist

Wood Duck, William D. Sarni; 1990. Native white pine, acrylic paint: h. 7 in. (17.8 cm) w. 13 in. (33 cm) d. 6 in. (15.2 cm). Carved in the style of Joseph W. Lincoln (1859-1938). Photo by artist

continue to create superb wood decoys in recognizable regional styles appreciated by collectors and hunters.

Ice Fishing Decoys

European settlers learned how to make and use fish decoys from Native American tribes. Though the Indians used bone, Europeans made theirs with carved, painted wood. Fishermen on the Great Lakes and waters of Michigan, Ohio, Minnesota, and Wisconsin were making and using carved ice fishing decoys by the 1850s to catch large, lake-dwelling fish, such as sturgeon, pike, and salmon. Lake Chautauqua, New York, was the earliest center of commercial spear fishing, and many fine decoys originated there.

In ice fishing, wintertime fishermen chop holes in lake ice and lower the decoys into the water, attracting live fish close enough to be speared. Decoys usually mimicked minnows, or fingerlings, such as trout or bass, appealing "dinner" for a bigger fish. Early decoys were given a metal tail and fins which could be curved to encourage the decoy to "swim" in a circle, plus a lead weight sinker, and a lead line attached to a jigging stick used to make the decoy move. (Chautauqua decoys usually had leather tails.) Ice fishing decoys vary in size from a few inches to several feet long. Some are highly abstract, while other have very realistic proportions, details, and colors. Decoys might also be very brightly colored or feature mirrors or glass eyes.

Professional craftsmen started making fish decoys around 1900, the peak years being 1920 to 1950. Oscar William Peterson (1887-1951) of Michigan was a hunting and fishing guide, and the pre-eminent maker of ice fishing lures. His decoys were particularly valued for their effective "action" in the water and are distinguished by long, thin bodies, slightly curved tails, bright colors, and detailed painting.

Fish Decoy, artist unknown, probably Michigan or Minnesota; 1930-1950. Painted wood, metal fins, metal base: h. 2¼ in. (5.7 cm) w. 5¼ in. (13.3 cm) d. 12¼ in. (31.1 cm). Collection of the Museum of American Folk Art, New York; gift of Elizabeth Ross Johnson. 1985.35.35

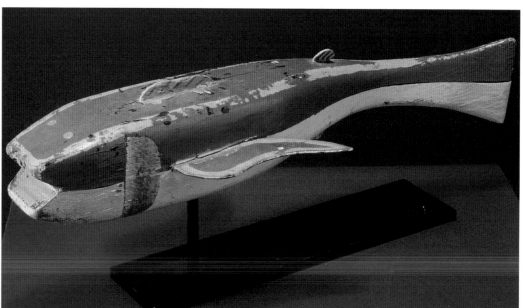

FIGURAL CARVING

Without detailing the many regional wood-carving traditions and individual carvers in American folk art, we can discern visual themes and references shared by all for hundreds of years. Religious imagery, as well as patriotic symbols and icons of America's founding and settlement (often romanticized), are very prominent. Flags, eagles, Lady Liberty, the Founding Fathers, Presidents, and other national heroes are popular.

Lady of Liberty, Alice Strom; 1999. Basswood, acrylic paint: h. 23 in. (58.4 cm) w. 19 in. (48.3 cm) d. 2½ in. (6.4 cm). Photo by artist

Sacred Heart, Nicholas Herrera; 1998. Watercolor, wood: h. 22½ in. (57.2 cm) w. 17½ in. (44.5 cm). Courtesy of Cavin-Morris Inc., New York

A third visual theme satirizes or comments on politics and social mores. Folk art carvings vary greatly in their degree of realism and technical skill. Carvers were often self-taught, and achieving a high level of technical polish simply wasn't part of their intent or important to the work.

Wilhelm Schimmel (1817-1890) was an eccentric, itinerant German sculptor who traveled throughout the Cumberland Valley in Pennsylvania, frequently ending up in jail or the almshouse. His work was well-known, and he traded his carvings when he could for room, board, and drink from the local German community. His sculptures were carved in soft pine, sealed with a white undercoat, then painted. His figures, principally of animals and birds, were highly stylized and frequently cross-hatched with chip-carving to mimic feathers or fur. Schimmel's techniques (not to mention his lifestyle)

Eagle with Outspread Wings, Wilhelm Schimmel (1817-1890), Carlisle, Pennsylvania; 1870-1890. Carved, gessoed, and painted pine: h. 20 in. (50.8 cm) w. 36⅝ in. (93 cm) d. 6½ in. (16.5 cm). Collection of the Museum of American Folk Art, New York; gift of Mr. And Mrs. Francis S. Andrews. 1982.6.10

have led some experts to categorize Schimmel as a tramp artist (see Outsider Art on page 75). The eagle was one of his favorite subjects. Schimmel's eagles often have their wings outspread; the wings were usually carved separately, then attached to the bodies with dowels or mortise work. Like Schimmel, there were many talented carvers of German origin in nineteenth-century Pennsylvania, including Aaron Mountz, whom Schimmel taught to carve.

Compared to the individuality of early American woodcarvers who often made their work according to a personal vision and without formal fine art training, other carvers produced works in a more polished, academic style that was in demand for public places and commercial purposes. When cigar smoking became popular in America in the 1800s, Americans copied English tobacconists and commissioned sculptors to make three-dimensional trade signs. The American Indian chieftain was a favorite symbol, given that native Americans introduced the colonists to tobacco. The same craftsmen who created ships' figureheads often made these magnificent, nearly life-sized figures, such as the Indian princess shown at left. Made

Indian Maiden Show Figure, attributed to Samuel Robb (1851-1928), New York; c. 1875-1900. Carved and painted wood: h. 56 in. (142.2 cm). Collection of the Museum of American Folk Art, New York; gift of Mrs. Gertrude Schweitzer. 1983.23.9

from white pine and kept brightly painted by merchants, the figures were displayed outside shop entrances. But by the 1890s, when cities became more densely populated, the figures were deemed obstructions to sidewalk traffic, and merchants were forced to remove them.

Toys, Whirligigs, and Whimsies

Toys are an important category of folk art carving in general. Most children played with homemade toys. In Christian homes where Sunday was strictly kept as the Sabbath day of rest and worship, some children were allowed to play with their Noah's Ark, a

"Sunday toy" used only on that day. Carved and brightly painted, the ark was constructed with a roof or doors that opened, and, of course, pairs of tiny animals. The toy neatly combined educational purpose and religious observance, a combination many Americans used to justify their pleasures. We are the Puritans' heirs, after all.

No one really knows when or where the whirligig originated in America. Based on the same mechanism as a windmill, these three-dimensional toys have parts that are designed to move or interact when driven by the wind, but they don't mark the wind's direction, only its velocity. Whirligigs were designed for pure pleasure, both for the amusement of its maker and viewers. Children ran holding whirligigs mounted on sticks, causing them to spin. Whirligigs were also mounted on fences or posts. The *Early Bird Catches the Worm* whirligig shown below is a fine example. Made of wood, metal, and/or found objects, whirligigs usually lack a high degree of surface finish or execution, but this is part of their pleasingly spontaneous appearance. There were various types of whirligig construction: figures with arms shaped like paddles to catch the wind; whirligigs with separate blades and pro-

pellers that catch wind power to make other parts move; whirligigs that feature bird, animal, and human figures; and whirligigs with entire vignettes of figures, buildings, and landscapes. Early creators particularly liked to poke fun at authority figures such as policemen or soldiers, whose dignity is severely compromised by their flailing arms! Whirligigs are still being actively made, as a drive in the country will probably show you.

Opposite page, right column: Noah's Ark (detail), Ted Nichols; 1992. Carved and painted wood: Ark h. 12 in. (30.5 cm) w. 16 in. (40.6 cm) d. ½ in. (1.3 cm). Photo by artist

Early Bird Catches the Worm, artist unknown, Northeastern United States; c. 1900. Carved and polychromed wood, wire: h. 42½ in. (108 cm) w. 36⅝ in. (93 cm) d. 16¼ in. (41.3 cm). Collection of the Museum of American Folk Art, New York; promised bequest of Dorothea and Leo Rabkin. P2.1981.5

painted ice fishing decoys

Even if the only place this aquatic quartet will swim is on your mantelpiece, it's fun to carve and paint them realistically enough so they look like lunch to other fish. That's what Great Lakes ice fishermen did during the winter to lure their catch to holes cut in the ice. A rainbow trout, a striped bass, a juvenile trout, and a wildly decorated sturgeon (made from an old chair leg!) complete this charming group.

David Vance, Designer

STRIPED BASS   RAINBOW TROUT

MATERIALS

– Patterns on page 140
– 1 x ³⁄₄-inch (2.5 x 1.9 cm) pine shelving cut to 8-inch (20.3 cm) lengths, one each for the trout and bass
– Turned chair leg, about 9 inches (22.9 cm) long, for the sturgeon
– Scrap of sheet copper or other lightweight metal
– 2 small plastic "eyes"*
– Copper rod, ³⁄₈-inch (9.5 mm) diameter and 4¹⁄₄ inches (10.8 cm) long, one for each fish (optional)
– Wooden blocks, 1¹⁄₄ x 3³⁄₄ x 3 inches (3.2 x 9.5 x 7.6 cm) for the sturgeon, and 1 x 4 x 1¹⁄₂ inches (2.5 x 10.2 x 3.8 cm) for the other fish (optional)
– Power drill with ³⁄₈-inch (9.5 mm) bit (optional)
*Available at craft stores

TOOLS AND SUPPLIES

– Handsaw
– Scissors
– Fine-tip permanent marker
– Pen knife, jackknife, or other type of carving knife
– Rasp and various grades of sandpaper, including fine
– Belt sander (optional)
– Die grinder with a sanding drum (optional)
– Tack cloth
– Flat acrylic paints in white, dark green (Pthalo green), metallic red, light green, metallic gold, red, and yellow
– Small artist's paintbrush
– Box cutter or craft knife
– White paper

JUVENILE TROUT

STURGEON

– Tin snips or shears
– Quick-drying epoxy
– Fine sandpaper
– Paint pens in black and gold
– Clear, satin finish spray-on acrylic enamel
– Ruler or measuring tape
– Wood stain or sealer (optional)
– Power drill with ⅜-inch (9.5 mm) bit

INSTRUCTIONS

1. Use the saw to cut an 8-inch (20.3 cm) piece of shelving for each fish you want to make (except for the sturgeon). Photocopy the patterns of your choice on page 140. Cut them out with the scissors, and use the permanent marker to trace around them onto the shelving pieces, creating an outline to guide your carving.

2. If you're making the rainbow trout, use the saw or knife to trim the tail to a thickness of about ¼ inch (6 mm).

3. Use the rasp and sandpaper or the belt sander to round down the corners and eliminate saw marks. Shape the fish more completely with rasp and sandpaper, or use the die grinder with the sanding drum.

4. Wipe off any dust with the tack cloth, then paint the fish with white acrylic paint. Let dry.

5. Using the box cutter or craft knife, cut into the wood about ¼ inch (6 mm) deep at the points you'll be placing the fins. Trace the fin patterns onto the paper, cut them out, then trace them onto the scrap copper. Cut them from the metal with the tin snips or shears.

Remember, you'll need four fins for the lower part of the fish.

6. Carefully place some of the quick-drying epoxy into the slits you cut in the wood for the fins, then insert the fins. Clean off any excess glue. Let dry.

7. Paint the fins white and let dry.

8. Use the fine sandpaper to lightly sand the painted wood. Wipe off any dust. Paint the trout dark green on top. Paint a red metallic stripe lengthwise along its middle, and paint the lower part of the fish light green, leaving the belly white. Let dry.

9. Paint the fins metallic gold and, while the paint is still wet, use the end of the brush to make rays in the fin that allow the green undercoat to show through. Let dry.

10. Use the black paint pen to make dots on the trout, placing them more heavily at the top and thinning them out toward the belly. Add gold dots to the dark green area. Let dry, then spray with the acrylic sealer to give a rich enamel look.

11. Follow the same basic procedure to create the striped bass from the pattern and wood and to cut out and attach the fins. Paint everything with a white base coat. Let dry, then paint the top two-thirds of the body and the fins with the light green paint. Thin the metallic gold paint with a tiny bit of water to make a wash and paint the white belly with it. Let dry, then use the black paint pen to make the gills, eyes, and mouth. Paint the body stripes and dorsal fins a dark green. Let everything dry, then use the black paint pen

to make the mouth, gills, dots on the body, and some rays on the dorsal fins. Let dry, then seal with the clear spray-on acrylic.

12. To make the juvenile trout, cut and shape the body, and cut and attach the fins. Carve a crescent-shaped gill slit on each side. Paint everything white, let dry, then paint the body yellow. Let dry, then use the red paint to make dots and to accent the mouth and gill slits. Use the paint pen to paint the fins black and to make the eyes, tail fin, and mouth.

13. To make the sturgeon, cut the chair rail to length with the band saw. Use the saw to make a vertical slit in the back end to insert the tail. Shape the tapering snout with the belt sander, or rasp and sandpaper. Trace the tail and fin patterns onto the copper, and cut them out. Use the box cutter to make the fin slits, then add epoxy and insert the fins and tail. Let dry. Paint the body white, let dry, then paint it green and let dry again. Now let your imagination go wild to add decorative painted accents to the body and head; dots within circles within circles are fun. Use the gold and black paint pens to make the rays in the fins and let dry. Spray the fish with the clear acrylic sealer and let dry. Epoxy the glass eyes in place. If you wish, bend the tail to the side to give it a slight curve, just like fishermen used to do so their lures would "swim" in a circle!

14. If you wish to display the fish on stands, finish the wood blocks with the stain or sealer, and let dry. Use the power drill with the $3/8$-inch (9.5 mm) bit to make a $1/2$-inch-deep (1.3 cm) hole in the midpoint of the belly of the fish. Drill a matching hole in the centerpoint of the block of wood. Insert the copper rod into the fish, then insert the other end of the rod into the wood block.

Noah's Ark

During colonial times, a Noah's Ark was the only toy some children were allowed to play with on the Sabbath. It shouldn't take you 40 days and 40 nights to make your own, however! Feel free to pick among colors, design elements, and patterns. If carpentry is new to you, or you haven't used wood shop tools before, get an experienced friend to help you.

Terry Taylor,
Designer

To build the ark:

MATERIALS

– Common white wood stock in the following dimensions:
– 2 x 6-inch board, 5 feet 12.7 cm) long;
  1 x 6 inch board, 6 feet (1.8 m) long; and
  a scrap of 2 x 2 board about 4 inches
  (10.2 cm) long

TOOLS AND SUPPLIES

– Ruler
– Pencil
– Table saw
– Carpenter's wood glue
– Adjustable wood clamps
– Safety goggles
– Band saw
– Router (optional)
– Sandpaper in a variety of
  grades, or a sanding sponge
– Handsaw
– Power drill and $^1/_{16}$-inch (1.6 mm) drill bit

– Wood filler
– Hammer
– Finishing nails

To make the figures and accessories:

MATERIALS

– 2 basswood strips, each $^1/_4$ inch (6 mm)
  wide and $6^3/_4$ inches (17.1 cm) long
– Wood dowel, $^1/_{16}$ inch (1.6 mm) diameter,
  12 inches (30.5 cm) long
– 2 small decorative wooden pegs
– Basswood or other white wood, $^3/_4$ inch
  (1.9 cm) thick, for the animals
– Scraps of basswood or balsa wood, $^1/_4$
  inch (6 mm) thick

TOOLS AND SUPPLIES

– Scissors
– Pencil
– Jigsaw
– Pocket knife or carving knife

To decorate the ark and figures:
– Acrylic base-coat paint
– Acrylic varnish
– Acrylic paint in colors of your choice
– Small artist's brushes
– Stencil or rubber stamp designs

INSTRUCTIONS

Building the Hull

1. Use the ruler, pencil, and saw to measure, mark, and cut three lengths of the 2 x 6 board, each 20 inches (50.8 cm) long. Spread the glue on the faces of the three boards, and stack them to create a thick block of wood. Clamp the stack with several of the adjustable clamps and let dry.

2. Draw a curved bow and stern on the glued wood block. Put on the safety goggles, and cut the shapes out with the band saw.

3. If desired, mark a $3\frac{3}{4}$ x $17\frac{1}{2}$-inch (9.5 x 43.2 cm) area for the deck, and use the router to carve it out.

4. Sand smooth any sharp edges.

Building the Cabin

1. Measure, mark, and use the saw to cut out the pieces for the cabin from the 1 x 6 board to the following dimensions: for the sides, two pieces measuring 5 x $11\frac{1}{2}$ inches (12.7 x 29.2 cm); for the gabled ends, two pieces measuring $\frac{5}{8}$ x 7 inches (1.6 x 17.8 cm); for the roof, two pieces measuring 4 x 12 inches (10.2 x 30.5 cm); for the roof cleat, one $\frac{1}{4}$ x 10- inch strip (6 mm x 25.4 cm); and one piece 3 inches square (7.6 x 7.6 cm).

2. Make a 30° bevel on a long side of each of the roof and side boards.

3. Mark and cut the front and back pieces with a 60° angle.

4. Bevel three sides of the 3 x 3-inch (7.6 x 7.6 cm) square with a 30° cut. Using a $\frac{1}{16}$-inch (1.6 mm) bit, drill a hole in the center of the square. Cut a short length of $\frac{1}{16}$-inch (1.6 mm) dowel, and glue it in the hole so a tiny bit sticks out.

Assembling the Ark

1. Glue, then nail, the sides to the gabled ends. Fill in all nail holes with the wood filler, let dry, and sand smooth.

2. Glue the cabin assembly to the deck of the hull. Toe in the finishing nails, hammering them in at an angle, to secure. Fill in and sand the nail holes.

3. Glue and nail the scrap of 2 x 2 to the deck and one gabled end of the cabin.

4. Glue and nail the 3 x 3 inch (7.6 x 7.6 cm) square on top of the 2 x 2 scrap.

5. Glue and nail one roof piece to the cabin.

6. Center the roof cleat on the inner side of the other roof piece. Center and tack the cleat $1\frac{1}{4}$ inches (3.2 cm) up from the long, square side of the roof. Set it on the cabin to check the fit, and adjust as needed, then glue and nail the cleat to the roof.

Decorating the Ark

1. Paint the ark with the acrylic base coat and let dry. Use the acrylic paints and brush to paint the hull cabin and roof as desired, adding painted windows and a door if you wish.

2. Use the stencils or rubber stamps to paint in a contrasting color to add decorative touches to the cabin. Let dry, and apply a final coat of the acrylic varnish to the ark.

Carving the Accessories

1. Photocopy the animal silhouettes on page

139. Cut them out, lay them on the basswood, and trace the outlines onto the wood. Draw two of each—except the dove and unicorn—and cut them out with the jigsaw.

2. Use the pocketknife to round the sharp edges, remove material between the legs or ears, and shape the heads. The carving doesn't need to be detailed because you can add detail with paint later. Since the figures are so general in nature, you can make a pair of horses from the unicorn pattern, or funny-looking dogs from the pig pattern.

3. Make the elephants' ears and deers' antlers by cutting the small scraps of basswood. Use scraps of the $\frac{1}{16}$-inch (1.6 mm) dowel to shape horns for the oxen and the unicorn. Use the tip of the knife to make channels or holes to fit the ears or antlers, and glue them in as desired. Use the tip of the knife to make a small hole in the base of the dove.

4. To make a ladder, cut two strips of the $\frac{1}{4}$-inch (6 mm) basswood, each $6\frac{3}{4}$ inches (17.1 cm) long. Measure and mark $\frac{3}{4}$-inch (1.9 cm) increments along the inner side of each strip.

5. Drill $\frac{1}{16}$-inch (1.6 mm) shallow holes on each mark.

6. Measure and cut the dowel into 1 inch (2.5 cm) lengths.

7. Glue the dowels in the holes between the basswood strips. Clamp and let dry.

8. Drill small holes on the side of the ark about 4 inches (10.2 cm) apart, sized to fit the two decorative pegs. Paint the pegs as desired and glue them in the holes.

Painting the Accessories:
1. Sand smooth the surfaces of the carved figures, and wipe off any dust.

2. Paint each figure with a coat of acrylic base coat and let dry. Paint each figure as desired with a color, let dry, and add details such as horn colors, fur stripes, or speckling for feathers. See the photographs for ideas. Let dry.

3. Give the figures a final, protective coat of acrylic varnish. Let dry. Position the dove on top of its dowel perch.

trusty sailor whirligig

WHETHER THE
NEAREST BODY OF
WATER IS AN OCEAN
OR A BIRDBATH, THIS
ENERGETIC LITTLE
FELLOW WILL MAKE
A FINE ADDITION TO
YOUR GARDEN. YOU
CAN ALSO POSITION
HIM INSIDE NEAR A
WINDOW TO ALERT
YOU TO ANY
INCOMING BREEZES.
YOU'LL LEARN
VALUABLE TIPS
ABOUT WOOD
CARVING WHEN YOU
MAKE THIS PROJECT.

RUSSELL SNOW,
Designer

MATERIALS

- Patterns on page 141
- Basswood or pine* in the following dimensions:
- For the body, one block $1\frac{1}{2}$ x $1\frac{1}{2}$ x $7\frac{1}{2}$ inches (3.8 x 4.4 x 19.1 cm)
- For the arms, two pieces $\frac{3}{4}$ x $\frac{3}{4}$ x 4 inches (1.9 x 1.9 x 10.2 cm) each
- For the base, one block $1\frac{1}{4}$ x $6\frac{1}{2}$ x 2 inches (3.2 x16.5 x 5.1 cm)
- For the stand, one piece $\frac{3}{4}$ x 4 x 4 x inches (1.9 x 10.2 x 10.2 cm)
- For the sailing ship, one piece 1/4 x 5 x 4 inches (6 mm x 12.7 x 10.2 cm)
- For the flags, two pieces $\frac{1}{8}$ x $1\frac{1}{2}$ x 1 inches (3 mm x 3.8 x 2.5 cm) each
- $\frac{1}{4}$-inch (6 mm) brass tube cut to the following lengths: $1\frac{7}{8}$ inch (4.7 cm) for the body sleeve; 3/4 inch (1.9 cm) for the base sleeve
- $\frac{3}{16}$-inch (4.8 mm) brass rod cut to the following lengths: for the axle, 3 inches (7.6 cm); for the stand, $2\frac{1}{2}$ inches (6.4 cm)
    - Small nail
    - Wood sealer
    - Latex exterior house trim paint or acrylic craft paints in white, black, gray, navy, red, brown, red, and flesh tone**
    - Clear acrylic sealer

*Basswood is more expensive than pine, but it's much easier to carve and is recommended for the body.

**Craft paints are available in small bottles at hobby and craft stores.

TOOLS AND SUPPLIES

- Power drill with $\frac{1}{4}$-, $\frac{3}{16}$-, $\frac{5}{32}$-, and $\frac{3}{32}$-inch (6, 4.8, 4, and 2.4 mm) bits
- Coping saw with a coarse blade
- Band saw or scroll saw (optional)
- Wood glue
- 2 paper clips
- Jeweler's blade (40 teeth per inch) for coping saw or scroll saw
- Small file or knife
- 1-inch (2.5 cm) belt sander (optional)
- Pencil
- Craft knife with #7 flat or #10 convex blade, and #28 concave blade
- Sandpaper, 100 and 220 grit
- Small paintbrush
- Liquid solution for expanding wood joints to fit tightly*
- Brass screws, two #6 x -$\frac{1}{2}$ inches (3.8 cm) and two #4 x $\frac{3}{4}$ inches (1.9 cm)
- Screwdriver
- Metal file
    *Available in hardware stores

INSTRUCTIONS

Drilling and Cutting

1. Begin by tracing the patterns on page 141 onto their respective wood pieces. To make the sailor's body, trace the side view first. Drill the $\frac{1}{4}$-inch (6 mm) arm sleeve hole and the $\frac{3}{32}$-inch (2.4 mm) foot holes before cutting the shape. Use the coping saw (or band or scroll saw, if you have one) to cut the shape of the side view. Now, trace the front view onto the block, and cut it out with the saw.

2. To make the arms, drill $3/16$-inch (4.8 mm) holes, $1/2$ to $5/8$ inch (1.3 to 1.6 cm) deep, in the two arm blanks. Cut the arm side view first. After cutting the front view, taper the last 1 inch (2.5 cm) of the arm about $1/4$ inch (6 mm) thick with a 30° angle as shown on the pattern. Glue the $1/8$-inch-thick (3 mm) flag pieces to the arms and use the paper clips to clamp them in place.

3. To make the boat, drill $3/32$-inch (2.4 mm) holes $3/8$ (9.5 mm) to $1/2$ inch (1.3 cm) deep where marked in the boat's bottom before cutting the shape. Try to cut with the grain of the wood.

4. Cut the base side view, then the top view. Drill a $1/4$-inch hole $3/4$ inch deep, to accommodate the brass sleeve. Drill $5/32$-inch (4 mm) foot screw holes all the way through, countersinking as indicated. Drill and countersink $3/32$-inch (2.4 mm) screw holes all the way through the arm of the base for the sailing ship.

5. Drill $3/16$-inch (4.8 mm) holes $1/2$ to $5/8$ inch (1.3 to 1.6 cm) deep in the stand, then cut the shape to the pattern.

6. Using the jeweler's blade on the scroll saw or coping saw, cut the $1/4$-inch (6 mm) brass tube to the lengths specified for the sleeves. Cut the $3/16$-inch (4.8 mm) rod to the lengths specified for the axle and stand. Remove any burrs inside the tubes with a small file or knife.

Carving

1. Before you start carving, remember that handmade crafts aren't meant to be perfect! If you're using the belt sander, cut the 1-inch (2.5 cm) 100-grit belt down the middle to create a $1/2$-inch (1.3 cm) belt. Rough out the body with the belt to save time. Before you round out the hat, cut away the top part of

the hat that's as wide as the side brims; this will create a square on top of the brim which can be rounded by knife or sander.

2. Use the pencil to sketch the face and collar on the wood. Use the craft knife with the concave blade to score the sketch to a depth that gives relief. Then, use either the flat or convex blade to remove the unwanted wood. It helps to do the face first. Be aware of the grain direction when you carve. Try to determine the direction of the grain, and carve so that you're "lofting," or carving up from the wood. Otherwise, the knife may follow the grain deeper into the wood than desired. Remove only small amounts of wood at a time. Fortunately, basswood is very forgiving.

3. Carve the sailor's bowed legs carefully. The grain runs such that you should carve the legs from the shoes to the knees and from the crotch to the knees. Rough out and carve the arms the same way.

4. If desired, carve or sand a chamfer or bevel on the top edge for extra visual interest, rounding the corners slightly.

Sanding
If you like the look of knife marks, sand the piece very lightly with 220-grit sandpaper. Sand a little harder if you want to remove the marks.

Painting
Use the brush to paint the pieces with the wood sealer, let dry,

then paint the piece with the house or acrylic paints as desired and let dry again. You might choose to paint semaphore flags instead of the American flag, or to give your sailor a striped shirt. If you want your whirligig to live outdoors, brush or spray on a coat of clear acrylic sealer.

Assembly

1. Insert the ¹/₄ x 1⁷/₈ inch (6 mm x 4.7 cm) brass sleeve through the body, leaving a small length sticking out at the shoulders. Insert the ¹/₄ x ³/₄-inch (6 mm x 1.9 cm) brass sleeve in the base, and press the nail up inside the sleeve to provide a bearing for the stand rod to turn upon. After putting four or more drops of the liquid joint expander into the hole, insert the ³/₁₆ x 2¹/₂-inch (4.8 mm x 6.4 cm) brass rod into the stand. The joint expander secures the brass rod to the wood by causing the wood to swell around the rod.

2. Position the body on the base so the base arm is to the left, allowing the arms to rotate. Secure the body to the base using the #6 x 1¹/₂-inch (3.8 cm) screws but don't over-tighten them.

3. Secure the boat to the base with the #4 x ³/₄-inch (1.9 cm) screws. The boat can face either direction.

4. Use the file to roughen about ¹/₂ inch (1.3 cm) of the smooth ends of the ³/₁₆ x 3-inch (4.8 mm x 7.6 cm) axle rod to provide grip on the arms. Take care not to remove too much metal, and file in the rod's lengthwise direction. Place four or more drops of the liquid joint expander into each arm hole, press the axle into one arm, insert in the sleeve, and press on the second arm 180° to the first. Be careful to leave some space between the arms and body so the arms can rotate. Spin the arms to see if they're well-balanced; it's not possible or necessary to achieve perfect balance, but you can rotate them slightly so they come to rest to your satisfaction. Let the liquid joint expander set about an hour.

5. Sign and date your whirligig, then fix it to a stand or display it as you like!

Tinsmithing and Tole Painting

Mary gave him a tin basin of water and a piece of soap, and he went outside the door and set the basin on a little bench there; then he dipped the soap in the water and laid it down; turned up his sleeves; poured the water on the ground, gently, and then entered the kitchen and began to wipe his face diligently on the towel behind the door. But Mary removed the towel and said:

"Now ain't you ashamed, Tom! You mustn't be so bad. Water won't hurt you."

Tom was a trifle disconcerted. The basin was refilled, and this time he stood over it a little while, gathering resolution; took in a big breath and began.

Mark Twain, *Adventures of Tom Sawyer,* 1876

Until the 1700s, early American colonists had to use earthenware, iron, wood, or pewter to make everyday household items. As a result, those objects tended to be heavy or bulky given the nature of their materials, and there were other drawbacks. Wood was hard to clean, iron rusted, and pewter contained poisonous lead. The introduction of tinware solved those problems: it was easy to clean, resisted rust when painted, and contained no lead.

Tinware originated in Europe, and tinsmithing emerged in the colonies in and around Berlin, Connecticut in the 1700s. Edward Pattison was one of the early Berlin craftsmen, and the town remained the industry center for more than 100 years. Very little tinware was used in the colonies until the late 1700s, and what existed was expensive and highly desired. Colonial tinsmiths used tinplate imported from England, and English law and export policy aimed at making it cheaper for colonists to purchase imported tinware rather than domestically made items.

St. Tammany Weathervane, artist unknown, East Branch, New York; late nineteenth century. Molded and painted copper: h. 102½ in. (260.4 cm) w. 103 in. (261.2 cm) d. 12 in. (30.5 cm). Collection of the Museum of American Folk Art, New York; Museum of American Folk Art purchase. 1963.2.1

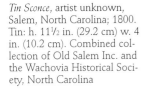

Tin Sconce, artist unknown, Salem, North Carolina; 1800. Tin: h. 11½ in. (29.2 cm) w. 4 in. (10.2 cm). Combined collection of Old Salem Inc. and the Wachovia Historical Society, North Carolina

Folk Art Tin Basket with Copper Bows, Robert D. Allio; 2000. Tin, copper: h. 9 in. (22.9 cm) w. 9½ in. (24.1 cm) d. 7 in. (17.8 cm). This twisted tin basket is made in a mid-nineteenth-century style. Photo by Claudene McClain

Tinplate was manufactured by dipping thin sheets of iron into liquid tin; the sheets could be cut, bent, and hammered into dozens of useful household and farm items. Inexpensive, lightweight, and shiny, the new "poor man's silver" quickly became popular among the middle and lower classes. The American tin industry expanded tremendously following the War of 1812 between England and America, when high tariffs on imported tin were lifted. In the first two decades of the 1800s, specialized machines that eliminated much of the handwork required by the craft were introduced, and contributed to the mass production of tin objects. By the mid-1800s, factory-made "Connecticut ware" and other mass-produced tinware were widely sold. Handmade tin had virtually disappeared by the early 1900s.

A tinsmith uses much the same tools as a blacksmith, though the tools are smaller and lighter. First the smith creates carefully sized patterns in sheet metal of the different pieces necessary to make an object. After scratching outlines of the patterns onto the sheet of tin (usually 11 x 15 inches [27.9 x 38.1 cm] or smaller), he uses metal shears to cut them

out. Tinplate is bent around anvils or other forms to create curves and angles; it does not need to be heated and beaten to be shaped, as does iron. Tinplate can be easily crimped, rolled, fluted, or punched with dimples, holes, or pinpricks before it is assembled. Pieces are attached by soldering; a specially shaped iron is heated and used to melt solder, a mixture of tin and lead, which grabs and holds the two pieces to be joined as it cools.

Watering Pitcher, Ed Vugteveen; 1996. Galvanized metal: h. 15½ in. (39.4 cm) w. 9 in. (22.9 cm) diameter. Photo by Martha Vugteveen

Tinsmiths sometimes copied designs originally made of more expensive materials, making them more affordable to people of modest means. Buyers could purchase tinware either unadorned, decorated with pierced holes, engraved with "wriggle-work" designs created with hammer and chisel, or decorated with engraving or paint. Sometimes the owner decorated her new acquisition herself (see Tole Painting on page 122).

Early tin kitchenware included coffeepots and teapots, pans, trays, and cookie cutters. The Pennsylvania Germans observed the Christmas season with a flurry of gingerbread-

Tin Cookie Cutters; artist unknown, Salem, North Carolina; nineteenth century. Tin: dimensions various. Combined collection of Old Salem Inc. and the Wachovia Historical Society, North Carolina.

Springerle Rolling Pin, John Vogler; 1824, Salem, North Carolina. Maple and hickory. Collection of the Wachovia Historical Society.

bakng and cookie-making. Intaglio-carved wooden springerle molds originated in Europe and were used to imprint stiff cake dough or marzipan with ornate patterns, but few people had time to carve the ornate molds. Out of economic necessity, the colonists used simple tin cookie cutters, and households exchanged different cutter shapes to enrich their repertoire. Favorites were animals, flowers, stars, hearts, diamonds, and gingerbread men.

Tin light fixtures were fabricated, including candleholders, sconces, lanterns, and candelabra. Lanterns were a particularly important item, used daily. Cylinders of perforated tin with a conical top and circular handle, lanterns also had perforations allowing the light of a candle to shine through. Other tin household items included trunks, baskets, and boxes intended to hold important documents, such as wills and deeds. Whimsical items were also crafted from tin, including miniature tokens presented on special occasions, such as wedding anniversaries; tiny top hats, shoes, books, irons, and umbrellas were among the objects made for amusement.

Little of the early American tinware survives today, unless it was varnished or painted.

Round Punched Tin Lantern with Three Windows, Robert D. Allio; 2000. Tin, handmade glass: h. 13½ in. (34.3 cm) w. 6 in. (15.2 cm) diameter. Photo by Claudene McClain. This lantern was made in the style of the mid-1800s.

Deed Boxes, Robert D. Allio; 2000. Tin: left h. 4½ in. (11.4 cm) w. 8¼ in. (21 cm) d. 4½ in. (11.4 cm); middle h. 6¼ in. (15.9 cm); right h. 3 in. (7.6 cm) w. 4 in. (10.2 cm) d. 2¾ in. (7 cm). Photo by Claudene McClain

Tole Painting

Many people think all painted tinware dating from colonial times was American in origin, but in fact it was largely imported from England during the 1700s. It was given the elegant-sounding name of "toleware" by Yankee peddlers. *Tole* is French for "tin," specifically referring to antique French ironware. Painted tinware was also called *japanned ware* because the colored decoration on a black background resembled Far Eastern lacquerware. Imported toleware was painted in mass production, and its graceful, asymmetrical brushwork looks quite different from the stiff symmetry of early colonial work.

Painted tinware, Rebekah L. Smith; 2000. Vintage metal canisters, acrylic paint. Dimensions various. These contemporary pieces are painted in a late nineteenth-century style.

From the late 1700s until the mid-1800s, painted tinware was extremely popular, and decorative treatments ranged from colorful amateur work to sophisticated japanning, which required the application of an asphaltum undercoat. A refined form of asphalt, asphaltum could be mixed with varnish and, when applied, gave a velvety smooth, black finish with a rich reddish to golden-brown sheen. The surface was then overpainted with stylized flowers, foliage, frills, and flourishes characteristic of nineteenth-century American painted tinware. The decorative technique of painting tin was so popular, it was also used on other metals such as copper, brass, and pewter.

The work of several well-known New England and New York tin shops are identifiable by details of their painted decoration, including the Filley shop (red balls), Upson shop (white scalloped bands), Buckley (red, green, and yellow borders), and Zachariah Stevens (realistic fruits and flowers with paints blended wet-on-wet). Women were often hired to paint tinware, or groomed within their tinsmithing families. The work of Ann Butler and her family in New York, for instance, is famous for its colorful, almost busy designs.

Weathervanes

Long before the advent of tinsmithing, the village blacksmith was a central figure in every early American settlement, because the objects he produced from iron were essential to nearly every aspect of life: hinges and nails for homes and furniture, implements for kitchen and hearth, and tools for shop and farm. Another type of object produced by early smiths may be the first thing many people think of when they think of folk art: the weathervane. Designed to provide settlers, farmers, and sailors with extremely important information on the weather, weathervanes were used as early as pre-Christian Greece and Rome. They incorporate moveable pointers that indicate the direction of the prevailing wind.

Weathervanes appeared in the first permanent settlements on America's eastern seaboard, and by the end of the 1700s they were commonly seen on homes, shops, government buildings, and churches. Early vanes were made of metal and of wood, but metal was more durable and therefore preferred; only a few wooden examples survive today.

In addition to their function as weather indicators, vanes were also treated decoratively, incorporating figures that could be clearly viewed against the sky. They were topped by flat silhouettes, such as the Archangel Gabriel shown at right. Angels were a popular motif, perhaps because of American religious revivals in the 1740s and a century later. Cut from wood or sheet metal, vane silhouettes were sometimes reinforced with metal pieces or bands. Some early weathervanes used Indian figures to indicate that the landowner had legitimately purchased the property from a local, native tribe. Designs reflected the commercial activities of the buildings topped by the vane, local occupations, and regional or national symbolism. Rural vanes featured domestic animals, such as roosters, horses, sheep, or cows; seaside vanes sported whales, ships, and other maritime motifs.

In the South, Anglophile colonists liked vanes with standards and banners. After the Revolutionary War and the centennial celebration in 1876, patriotic motifs flourished around the United States, including the eagle, George Washington, the figure of Columbia, and the newly erected Statue of Liberty. For his home at Mount Vernon, Virginia, Washington himself commissioned Joseph Rakestraw of Philadelphia to make the mansion's "Dove of Peace" weathervane in 1787.

During the last quarter of the 1800s, copper became the favored weathervane material because the metal was durable and easy to work. It was easier to make figures in relief

Archangel Gabriel Weathervane, artist unknown, United States; c. 1840. Painted sheet metal: h. 35 in. (88.9 cm) w. 32½ in. (82.6 cm) d. 1¼ in. (3.2 cm). Collection of the Museum of American Folk Art, New York; gift of Mrs. Adele Earnest. 1963.01.01

or in three dimensions in copper, such as the famous St. Tammany Indian weathervane shown on page 119. It stood for many years on top of a political clubhouse in East Branch, New York, in the western Catskill Mountains.

Commercial weathervane companies arose in New York City, Philadelphia, and Boston in the mid-1800s. Processes for casting iron or molding copper were mechanized and standardized. Molds shaped sheet copper into two "halves" of a three-dimensional vane, which were then soldered together. Finishing details and textures were added by hand and hammer. As the technologies of mass production were refined, however, vane designs were simplified to accommodate the limitations of stamping metal with machines, and individual handcraft was completely eliminated from the manufacturing process. After 1850, most metal weathervanes were mass produced.

wall candle sconce

NOTHING COULD BE MORE EVOCATIVE OF COLONIAL DAYS THAN THE WARM GLOW OF CANDLELIGHT, AND THE SIMPLE SHAPE OF THIS SCONCE HAS ITS OWN QUIET BEAUTY. WORK SLOWLY AND ACCURATELY WHEN YOU COPY AND CUT OUT THE PATTERN PIECES, SO THE PARTS OF THE SCONCE WILL FIT TOGETHER TIGHTLY, AND BE CAREFUL OF SHARP EDGES. IF YOU DON'T WANT TO DO THE SOLDERING YOURSELF, TAKE THE PIECES TO A LOCAL WELD SHOP.

MICHAEL J. SAARI,
Designer

MATERIALS

– Patterns on page 126
– 24-gauge sheet tin, 16 x 20 inches (40.6 x 50.8 cm)
– Taper candle

TOOLS AND SUPPLIES

– Scissors
– Masking tape or rubber cement
– Awl or scribing tool
– Fine-tip permanent marker
– Safety goggles
– Protective gloves
– Straight tin snips
– Curved tin snips
– Ruler
– Vise
– Hammer with plastic or wooden head
– Flat-head screwdriver
– Standard hammer
– Block of soft pine wood
– PVC pipe, 2-inch (5.1 cm) diameter
– Denatured alcohol
– Rags
– Heat-resistant work surface
– String, tape, or No. 20 black iron binding wire (optional)
– Heat-resistant work surface
– Soldering flux (optional)
– Flux brush (optional)
– Electric soldering iron (optional)
– Soft (also called *common*) solder (optional)
– Wooden dowel, $7/8$-inch (2.2 cm) diameter
– Metal punch, $5/8$-inch (1.6 cm) diameter*, or a piece of metal pipe with one end ground to a sharp edge
– Hammer
  *Available in hardware or industrial supply stores

INSTRUCTIONS

1. Photocopy the patterns on page 126, enlarging 222 percent, and cut them out with the scissors. Place the patterns on the tin sheet, securing them with the tape or rubber cement, and use the awl to scribe around them very carefully, etching their outlines onto the tin. Use the permanent marker or awl to indicate the punch hole locations.

2. Put on the safety goggles and gloves. Use the straight and curved tin snips to cut out the pieces. Use the straight snips to cut straight lines and corners, and the curved snips to cut curves or circles. When cutting sheet metal, the key is never to close the blades completely as you make a cut. Before the blades close all the way, open the snips and guide fresh metal back into the blades, never taking the snips out of the cut. When cutting an outlined shape, it's easier to cut it out with a surrounding margin of metal first, then trim it just to the right of the outline.

3. Now you'll make folded edges on the left and right sides of the sconce back plate. Use the ruler and marker to mark a $1/4$-inch (6 mm) margin on both edges. Secure the marked edge in the vise, making sure it's straight. By small increments, bend the edge to a 90° angle. Remove from the vise, and repeat the process to create the other folded edge.

4. Lay the sconce back on the work surface, and use the plastic- or wooden-headed hammer to completely flatten the folded edges. The side with the folded edges will serve as the back of the sconce.

5. Place the sconce base piece flat on the soft pine block. Measure and mark a $1/4$-inch (6 mm) margin on the straight back edge of the base, and bend it down 90° to create a flat surface for soldering the base to the back plate (but don't solder it yet).

6. Now you'll form the rim of the sconce base. Mark, fold, and flatten a $1/4$-inch (6 mm) edge on the rim piece as you did in steps 3 and 4.

7. Use the PVC pipe to gradually form a curve in the rim piece to fit the arc of the sconce base. Use the ruler and permanent marker to indicate ³/₁₆-inch (4.8 mm) margins at each end of the rim, then bend them 90° to attach them to the back of the back plate.

8. After carefully cleaning all the surfaces with a rag moistened with the denatured alcohol, and securing them in a good surface-to-surface join with the tape or wire, solder the rim to the base, and the back plate to the base.

9. Measure, mark, and make a ¹/₈-inch (3 mm) fold along the edge of the candle tube piece that has notched corners. Place the piece on the soft pine block and use the plastic- or wooden-headed hammer to flatten the fold.

10. Form the candle tube by bending it over the wooden dowel until the tube has a ⁷/₈-inch (2.2 cm) inner diameter, checking the measurement with the ruler. Center the tube on the sconce base, and use the awl to make slight marks where the tabs will slot in. With the sconce base flat on the work surface, use the flat-head screwdriver and regular hammer to punch the slots in the sconce base.

11. Insert the candle tube prongs through the slots you punched in the base, then bend over the tabs so they're flat against the underside. Clean the metal, secure, and solder the tabs to the base, then solder the candle base to the back plate.

12. Place the sconce with its back flat on the pine block, and use the metal punch or the sharpened metal pipe and hammer to punch the mounting hole at the top of the sconce. The more you hammer, the larger the hole will be.

13. Use the rags and alcohol to clean all of the soldered joints. Insert the taper candle in the candle tube.

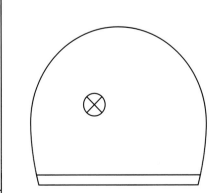

Enlarge all pattern pieces 222%

 Tin cookie cutters

There's hardly anything that reminds us so eloquently of home and hearth as homemade cookies. Using cookie cutters you made yourself can add an even more personal touch. They also make charming wall accents when not in use. Have an experienced friend help you with the soldering, or take the pieces to a local weld shop.

Michael J. Saari,
Designer

Materials

– Piece of sheet tin, 8 x 20 inches (20.3 x 50.8 cm)
– Patterns on page 138 and 139

Tools and Supplies

– Scissors
– Rubber cement (optional)
– Awl or scribing tool
– Ruler
– Pencil
– Protective gloves
– Safety goggles
– Straight tin snips
– Curved tin snips
– Small pliers
– Denatured alcohol
– Rags
– Heat-resistant work surface**
– C-clamps or spring-type clamps
– Lead-free solder*
– Flux
– Flux brush
– Electric soldering gun, or a nonelectric soldering iron (called a copper) plus a small, handheld propane torch*
– Matches or lighter (if working with a torch)
– Piece of scrap board
– Hammer with large, flat striking face
– Screwdriver
– PVC or metal pipe, 2-inch (5.1 cm) diameter
  *Available at plumbing supply houses and hardware stores
  **Metal-covered asbestos oven pads work perfectly and are available at kitchen supply stores.

Instructions

1. Photocopy the cutter and handle patterns. Cut them out and lay them on the tin sheet. To keep them in place, you may want to brush some rubber cement on one side. Use the awl or scribe to trace around the pattern, etching the outline in the tin, plus any punch marks. Remove the pattern. Measure and mark a $\frac{5}{8}$ x 20-inch (1.6 x 50.8 cm) strip with the ruler and pencil on the tin, and scribe it, too. It will serve as the edge of one cookie cutter.

2. Put on the protective gloves and goggles. Use the tin snips to cut out the patterns. Use the straight snips to cut straight lines and corners, and the curved snips to cut curves or circles. When cutting sheet metal, the key is never to close the blades completely as you make a cut. Before the blades close all the way, open the snips and guide fresh metal back into the blades, never taking the snips out of the cut. When cutting an outlined shape, it's easier to cut it out with a surrounding margin of metal first, then trim it just to the right of the outline.

3. Lay the cutout pattern flat on your work surface, and use the pliers to start bending the long, cutout strip of metal to follow the pattern. Once you've partly formed the cut-

Photo 1

ter edge, you can tack-solder it to the cookie pattern in selected points to hold it in place. The cutter edge should be about $3/16$ to $1/4$ inch (4.8 to 6 mm) in from the outside edge of the cutter pattern (see photo 1).

4. To solder, clean the metals thoroughly with the rag and alcohol. Working on the heat-resistant surface, clamp the two pieces together, and apply the flux generously to the points where they'll be joined. Flux the tip of the electric iron or copper, and heat it. Reflux the tip and melt a bit of solder on it. Hold the tinned point against the join of the metal to heat it, then hold a piece of solder against the join close to the iron. Immediately move the iron along the joint, pulling the solder along behind it. Let the solder cool completely before moving it, or it may not hold.

5. Continue to bend, shape, and tack-solder the cutter edge to the pattern. If there's an extra edge after you've finished forming it, use the snips to cut the excess off. Now solder the entire edge of the cutter to the pattern.

6. Lay the cookie pattern face down on the piece of wood, with the cutter side up. Use the screwdriver and hammer to punch decorative holes in the pattern at the points indicated.

7. Now you'll form the handle. To finish the edges of the cut piece, use the pliers to bend and fold over a $3/16$-inch-wide (4.8 mm) margin along each long side, then carefully hammer it flat. Bend the handle over the 2-inch (5.1 cm) PVC pipe to form a half-round shape. Use the pliers to bend up $3/16$-inch (4.8 mm) tabs at each end of the handle. Clean the metal, and solder the handle to the cookie pattern (see photo 2). Remove any solder flux by rubbing it with the rag moistened with alcohol.

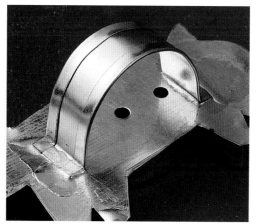

Photo 2

Painted Tin Document Box

MATERIALS

– Document box in tin or other metal*
– Patterns on page 132
– Rust-preventive spray primer in flat red
– Acrylic craft paints in black, red, off-white, mustard, and medium green
  *You can find old metal boxes in junk stores, or use modern reproductions found in craft stores

TOOLS AND SUPPLIES

– Fine sandpaper or scouring pads (optional)
– Assorted small paintbrushes, including fine-tipped artist's brushes
– Masking tape
– Ruler
– Patterns on page 132
– Tracing paper
– Pencil
– Carbon paper
– Protective rubber gloves
– Clean rag
– Gel wood stain in walnut or antiquing rub

INSTRUCTIONS

1. If there are any rusty spots on the metal, knock them off by sanding lightly with the sandpaper or pad.

2. Spray on the primer, and let dry thoroughly.

3. Use a brush to paint the entire box with the black paint. This will serve as the base coat. Let dry.

4. Refer to the photographs on page 132. Use the masking tape to tape off the border of the lid rim, then paint the border red. Let dry. Use the ruler and pencil to mark a 1½-inch (3.8 cm) border on the box body, then mask off the area with tape and paint it white. Let dry, then remove the tape.

5. Use a photocopier to enlarge the patterns on page 132 to fit your box. Now you'll transfer the pattern to the white band on the box. Use the pencil and tracing paper to trace the pattern, then slip carbon paper between the tracing and the box. Secure with masking tape, then go over the pattern with the pencil, transferring the carbon outlines to the box surface.

6. Repeat step 5 to transfer the pattern on page 132 to the red lid band, and the front, sides, and back borders of the box.

7. Following the colors shown in the photographs, you'll now paint over the patterns on the box borders and lid. Use simple brush strokes, and don't overload your paintbrush with paint. Let dry.

8. Measure in ¾ inch (1.9 cm) from the edge of the box, and mark off the red borders in pencil. The borders should be ⅛ inch (3 mm) wide.

9. Repeat step 5 to transfer the central pattern on page 132 to the box front, along with the lid corner patterns and handle motif.

10. Paint the central design and let dry. Mask off the red border lines with tape, paint them, and let dry. Paint all the borders and the designs on the lid, and let dry. Again, don't overload your brush. You can also give the leaf and scroll forms the illusion of vol-

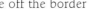

THESE DAYS WE USE BANKS, BUT, IN CENTURIES PAST, PEOPLE OFTEN STORED DEEDS, RECORDS, AND IMPORTANT RECEIPTS IN TIN DOCUMENT BOXES AT HOME. AFTER YOU DECORATE YOUR BOX WITH EASILY-PAINTED, TRADITIONAL PATTERNS, WHY NOT USE IT TO HOLD YOUR FAVORITE RECIPES, OR AS A UNIQUE TEA CADDY?

REBEKAH L. SMITH,
Designer

ume by painting a simple line on one side and a line down the middle of the form, using the same paint lightened a bit by mixing in a little white paint. Let dry. Save the "dot" details for last; create them by dipping the end of a straight artist's brush into the white paint, and dabbing it straight onto the surface. Let dry.

11. After the paint is thoroughly dry, put on the rubber gloves and use the rag to rub a moderate amount of the wood stain onto the box. (Be sure to work in a well-ventilated area.) Let the stain stand for one minute, then rub it off to achieve the coloring you desire. Let dry.

Lid corners

Handle Motif

TINSMITHING AND TOLE PAINTING

Trumpeting Angel Weathervane

This elegant weather-vane is constructed much like the earliest weathervanes, which were two-dimensional figures cut from metal. Because you're using copper, you can use hand tools to shape the metal and a handheld propane torch to heat it. If you prefer, take the cut-out pieces to a local metal fabricator and have them do the bending, riveting, and soldering.

MICHAEL J. SAARI,
Designer

MATERIALS

– Copper sheet, .05 inch thickness approximately equivalent to 14-gauge or $1/16$ inch [1.6 mm], 30 x 30 inches (76.2 x 76.2 cm) square
– Pattern on page 139
– Copper reinforcing stock, $1/8$ inch (3 mm) thick, $3/4$ inch (1.9 cm) wide, $7\frac{1}{2}$ feet (2.1 m) long
– 27 copper rivets, $3/16$-inch (4.8 mm) diameter
– Copper tubing, $3/4$-inch (1.9 cm) diameter, 16 inches (40.6 cm) long
– 2 copper rivets, $1/4$-inch (6 mm) diameter
– Ready-made compass directional (optional)*
– $3/4$-inch (1.9 cm) copper tube, 15 inches (38.1 cm) long
– $3/4$-inch (1.9 cm) stainless steel round solid stock in length determined by the site location**
– $3/4$-inch (1.9 cm) ball bearing***

*Cast directionals are available from ornamental iron and architectural suppliers.

**If you plan to mount your weathervane on a roof, the shaft should be a minimum of 3 feet (0.9 m) long from the weathervane to the roof peak, and extend another 1 to 3 feet (30 cm to 0.9 m) inside the roof for attachment, making a total length of 4 to 6 feet (1.2 to 1.8 m)

***Available from industrial suppliers

TOOLS AND SUPPLIES

– Scissors
– Fine-tip permanent marker, awl, or scribing tool
– Safety goggles
– Protective gloves
– Compass saw or jigsaw with fine-toothed cutting blade
– C-clamps or vise grips
– Electric drill with $13/64$, $1/4$, and $5/16$-inch (5, 6, and 8 mm) drill bits
– Hand-held propane torch*
– Lighter or flint striker
– Heavy-duty tongs
– Ball-peen or cross-peen hammer
– Steel-covered bench or anvil
– Sandpaper, 150 grit
– Steel wool or synthetic scouring pads
– Ruler or measuring tape
– Hacksaw
– Flat file
– Metal shears
– Denatured alcohol
– Rags
– Soldering flux
– Flux brush
– Soldering iron
– Soft (also called *common*) solder
– 2 set screws, $5/16$ inch (8 mm) diameter
– Handheld compass

*Available in home improvement centers and plumber's supply stores

INSTRUCTIONS

1. Use a photocopier or grid paper and pencil to enlarge the pattern on page 139, marking the locations of the drill holes. Cut out the pattern and place it on the copper sheet; it will fit if you position it diagonally on the piece of metal. Use the permanent marker or awl to transfer the pattern, including the locations for rivets, reinforcing bars, and the angel's eye to the copper.

2. Put on the safety goggles and gloves. Using the compass saw or jigsaw, cut out the pattern. Clamp the copper to the work surface, and use the $1/4$-inch (6 mm) drill bit to drill out the angel's eye where marked on the pattern.

3. Use the piece of wire or string to measure the length of each of the reinforcing bars indicated on the weathervane pattern, following their curves. Lay the string on the

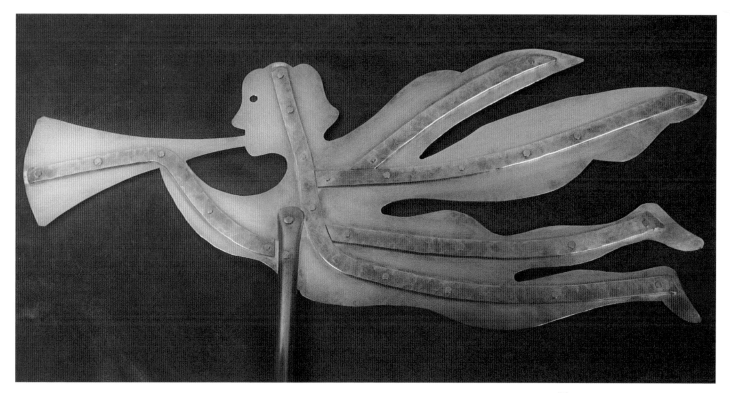

Photo 1

reinforcing bar stock, and use the marker or awl to mark the length plus 2 inches (5.1 cm). Use the compass saw or jigsaw to cut the reinforcing bars from the $^1/_8$ x $^3/_4$ inch (3 mm x 1.9 cm) copper stock to length. The bars will stiffen the sheet copper and add a slightly three-dimensional quality (see photo 1). Use the permanent marker or awl to mark the drill hole positions on the bars.

4. The bars will have to be heated and bent to the shape of the figure. Working on a fire-proof surface, light the propane torch and use it to heat the bar to a dull red, then bend the bar to fit the areas specified on the pattern. Bend the hot bar to shape with the tongs and hammer, then flatten it by placing it on the steel-covered bench or anvil and hammer it, achieving a nicely dimpled surface effect. Repeat with each bar.

5. Use the saw to trim any excess length from the reinforcing bars.

6. Clamp each bar to the table, and drill $^1/_8$-inch (3 mm) holes where marked. Position the bars on the copper cutout, and mark the drill holes. Remove the bars, and drill $^1/_8$-inch (3 mm) holes in the cutout, using the drill to ream out the holes slightly. You'll drill a total of 27 holes.

7. Clean all the metal surfaces using the 150-grit sandpaper, then go over them again with the scouring pads or steel wool. Reposition the bars on the cutout, matching up the drilled holes.

8. The rivets will have a machined head on one end. Fit the $^3/_{16}$-inch (4.8 mm) rivets through the holes, with the "head" of the rivet on the right side of the weathervane and protruding about $^3/_{16}$ inch (4.8 mm) above the surface. With the weathervane resting right side down on the steel work surface, use the ball end of the ball-peen hammer to hit the end of the rivet sticking out the wrong side. The machined end should spread slightly (called *peening over*) into a "mush-

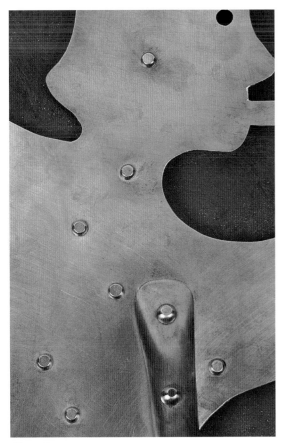

Photo 2

room" shape. You may have to go back and forth, hammering one side and then the other, to ensure the rivet is seated tightly.

9. Now you'll make the shaft for the weathervane. Use the ruler or measuring tape to measure 3 inches (7.6 mm) in from one end of the 16-inch (40.6 cm) piece of copper tubing, and mark with the permanent marker. Use the hacksaw to saw a slit down the middle of that end. Slip in a piece of the same copper sheet you used to cut out the weathervane, big enough to fill the slit and leave some margin around the tube, and use the hammer to flatten the end (see photo 2).

10. Remove the piece of scrap copper, and use the flat file to file the shaft at the 3-inch (7.6 cm) slit, creating a fork. Slip the angel cutout into the fork.

11. Use the C-clamps to secure the cutout and shaft to the work surface. Drill two 1/4-inch (6 mm) holes at the end of the shaft, the first one about 3/4 inch (1.9 cm) below the end and the second hole about 2 inches (5.1 cm) beneath the first hole.

12. Insert the two 1/4-inch (6 mm) copper rivets in the holes so they protrude 1/4 inch (6 mm), and use the hammer to rivet them in place so they peen over.

13. The compass directional shown in the photograph was ready-made, but you can make your own by drawing the letters N, S, E, and W on the sheet copper and cutting them out with metal shears. Cut pieces of 1/8 x 3/4-inch (3 mm x 1.9 cm) flat copper stock to lengths that please you, and weld or solder them to the 3/4-inch (1.9 cm) copper tube shaft of the weathervane, or take them to a weld shop and have them do it.

14. Drill two 5/16-inch (8 mm) holes in the copper tube, and insert the two 5/16-inch (8 mm) set screws. You'll use the screws to secure the directional to the shaft. If you use a ready-made directional, simply loosen its set screws enough to slide it up over the weathervane shaft, then tighten the screws.

15. The 3/4-inch (1.9 cm) stainless steel, round solid stock will serve as the mounting shaft for the entire weathervane, with its length determined as specified above. Sink the vane into the ground of your garden, or hire a professional, if you want to secure it to a roof.

16. Once the shaft is securely installed, slide the compass over the shaft, checking its orientation with the compass. After you've fixed the "N" in a northerly direction, the angel will spin with the directionals. Tighten the set screws, then drop the 3/4-inch (1.9 cm) steel round bearing into the pivot shaft, and carefully slide the copper weathervane shaft over it. Make sure there's a minimum 1/2-inch (1.3 cm) clearance between the directionals and the angel so the weathervane can spin. If it's exposed to the weather, the copper will acquire a beautiful greenish-blue patina with time.

patterns

Twisted Tin Can Chair Trio

■ Connector

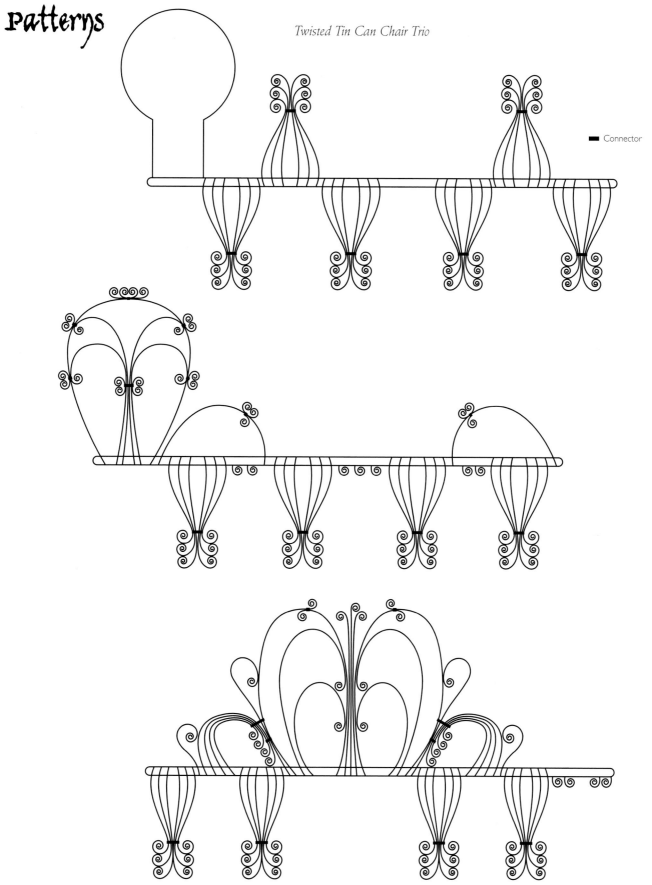

Strippy Quilt

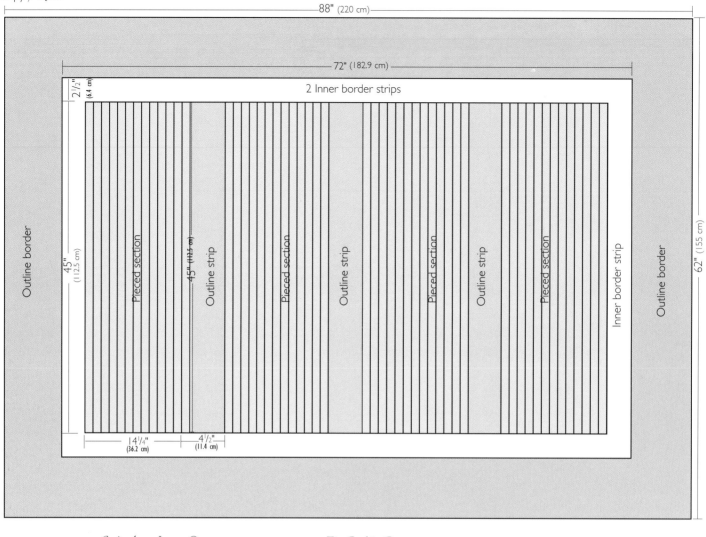

Scrimshaw Letter Openers   *Tin Cookie Cutters*

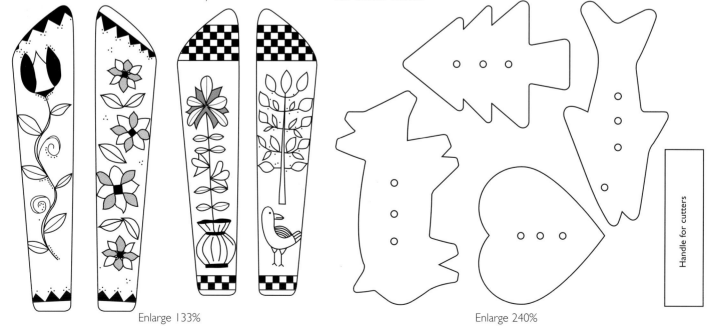

Enlarge 133%

Enlarge 240%

Birch Bark Canoe

Enlarge 190%

Noah's Ark

Enlarge all 166%

Ear

Tin Cookie Cutters

Trumpeting Angel Weathervane

Enlarge 700%

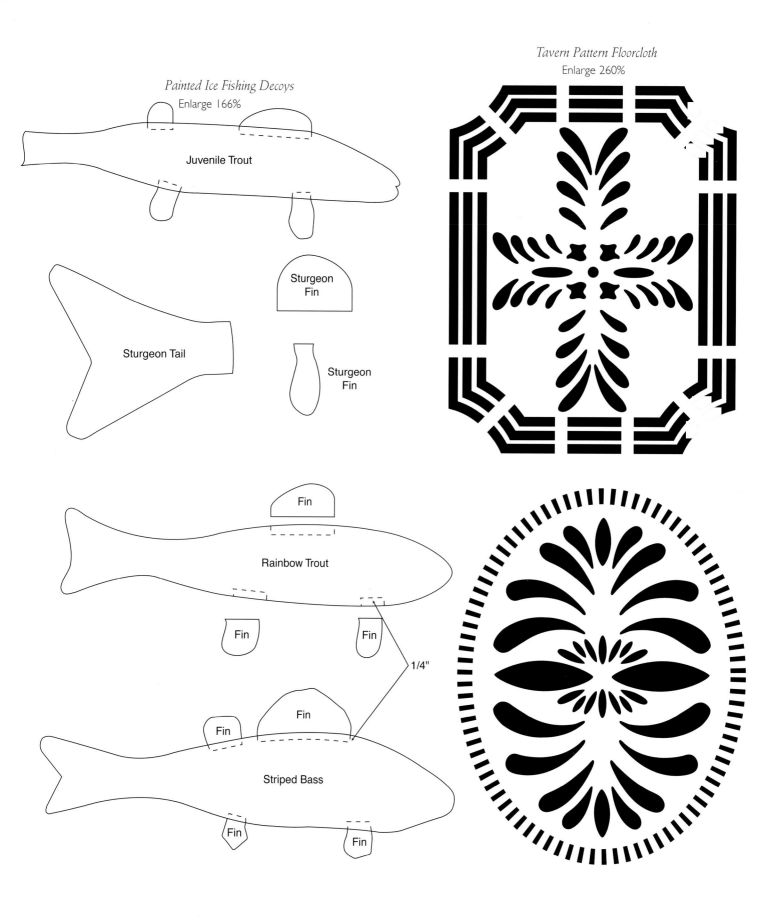

Painted Ice Fishing Decoys
Enlarge 166%

Juvenile Trout

Sturgeon Tail

Sturgeon Fin

Sturgeon Fin

Fin

Rainbow Trout

Fin

Fin

1/4"

Fin

Fin

Striped Bass

Fin

Fin

Tavern Pattern Floorcloth
Enlarge 260%

Trusty Sailor Whirligig

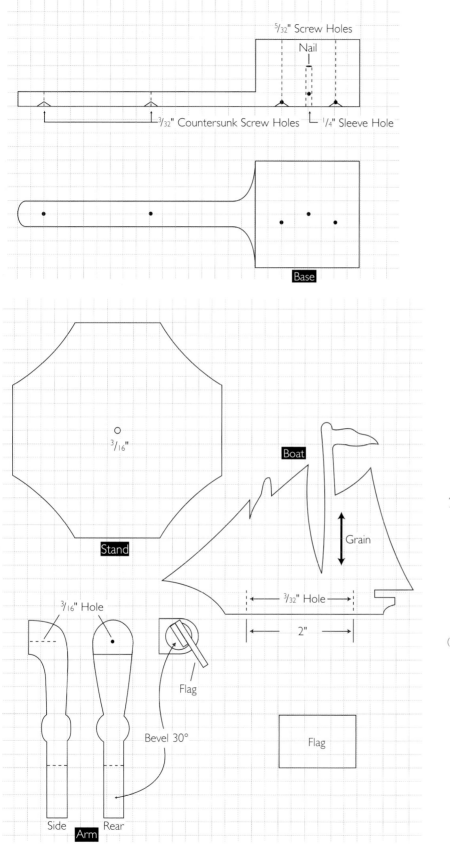

⁵/₃₂" Screw Holes

Nail

³/₃₂" Countersunk Screw Holes — ¹/₄" Sleeve Hole

Base

Stand

³/₁₆"

Boat

Grain

³/₁₆" Hole

Flag

Bevel 30°

³/₃₂" Hole

2"

Flag

Side   Rear

Arm

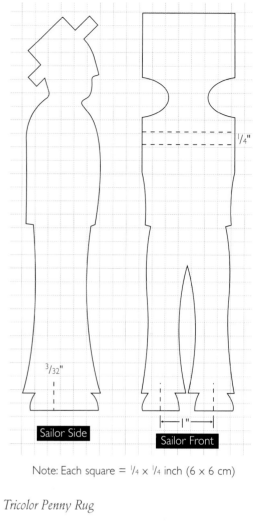

¹/₄"

³/₃₂"

Sailor Side

1"

Sailor Front

Note: Each square = ¹/₄ × ¹/₄ inch (6 × 6 cm)

Tricolor Penny Rug

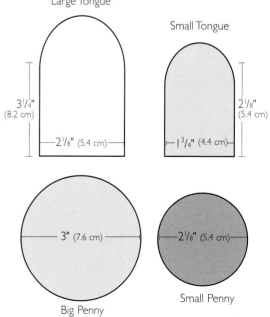

Large Tongue

3¹/₄"
(8.2 cm)

2¹/₈" (5.4 cm)

Small Tongue

2¹/₈"
(5.4 cm)

1³/₄" (4.4 cm)

Big Penny

3" (7.6 cm)

Small Penny

2¹/₈" (5.4 cm)

Enlarge to measurements indicated

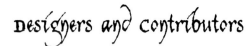 Designers and contributors

Greg Adams designs and builds rustic furniture. 702 Main Street, Lapel, IN 46501, (765) 534-3009.

Robert D. Allio makes original tin items and historic reproductions from his business, Cooperstown Tinker Shop. RD #1, Box 11, Cooperstown, PA 16317, (814) 374-4048.

Kathy Barrick-Dieter designs and markets original and historical needlework patterns. Barrick Samplers, 337 Radcliffe Avenue, Hagerstown, MD 21740. <kbdieter@aol.com>

Todd Barrow designs and builds rustic furniture that is showcased in galleries and homes throughout the Southeast. Rustic Raven, P.O. Box 121, Mars Hill, NC 28754, (828) 689-9672. <raven@madison.main.nc.us>

Dennis Belanger and his wife Sheila create seventeenth-through nineteenth-century reproduction floorcloths, and also market period furnishings and accessories. Early American Floorcloths, 28 Ledgewood Road, Claremont, NH 03743, (603) 543-3663. <www.floorcloths.net>

Nancy A. Braski gathers natural plant materials to make her award-winning baskets, which have been featured in national publications and at craft fairs and galleries. 273 Arrowhead Trail, Kingston, TN 37763, (865) 376-4795. <braski@icx.net>

Irene Semanchuk Dean exhibits her work at galleries and at craft shows and is the author of *The Weekend Crafter-Polymer Clay* (Lark Books, 2000). <www.good-night-irene.com>

Susan Feller specializes in early nineteenth-century primitive hooked rugs. Ruckman Mill Farm Hooked Rugs, P.O. Box 409, Augusta, WV 26704. (908) 832-9565. <www.ruckmanmillfarm.com>

Janet Flinchbaugh specializes in custom floorcloths and historical replicas. The Pine-Apple Tree, 13 Cunningham Avenue, Glen Falls, NY 12801, (518) 793-5571.

Barry Gregson is a rustic furniture maker. Charlie Hill Road, RR Box 88, Schroon Lake, NY 12870, (518) 532-9384.

Nicholas Herrera is a New Mexico native whose sculpture appears in collections including the Smithsonian National Gallery of American Art. Cavin-Morris Gallery, 560 Broadway, New York, NY 10012, (212) 226-3768.

Wendy G. Jensen makes traditional and utilitarian rattan baskets. Berkshire Basketry, 25 Christian Hill Road, Great Barrington, MA 01230, (413) 528-4007.

Karl Johnson creates hand-cut silhouette portraits at a variety of venues all over the world. Johnson also makes portraits by mail order and is a member of the Village of Yesteryear Guild. 5428 Saloma Avenue, Sherman Oaks, CA 91411, (704) 293-6432. <villageofyesteryear.com>

Linda L. Kerlin creates needlework in various forms in her restored 18th-century log cabin home. Log Cabin Homestead, 2084 Mt. Gretna Road, Elizabethtown, PA, 17022; (717) 367-1812. <llklogcabin@aol.com>

Diane Killeen is certified in restoration technique and faux painting by the City of London and its professional guilds. She creates custom works of art on walls, furniture, and canvas. Just Paint It!, 100 Griffing Boulevard, Asheville, NC 28804, (828) 236-0724.

Rick Ladd is an artist and craftsman inspired by folk craft traditions, particularly bottlecap work and the whimsical, inventive qualities of folded paper prison art. 561 47th Street, Brooklyn, NY, 11220; (718) 972-0821. <bottlecap@mindspring.com>

Claudia W. Leo is a basketmaker. She is represented in the Smithsonian Museum of American History. Potowmack Basket Works, 5344 Cristfield Court, Fairfax, VA 22032, (703) 323-9096.

Anne Leslie creates profile

shadow portraits from one-minute sittings and photographs. The Paper Paintbrush, (703) 960-0095. <www.shadowportraits.com>

Dan Mack is a self-taught woodworker and highly sought after teacher, lecturer, and designer. He is author of several Lark Books on rustic furniture. Rustic Furnishings, 14 Welling Avenue, Warwick, NY 10990, (914) 986-7293.

Janice Maddox makes quilts in the mountains of Western North Carolina. 700 Chunns Cove Road, Asheville, NC 28805. (828) 254-9103. <jkmdx@hotmail.com>

Lisa Curry Mair creates colonial and folk art floorcloths. Canvasworks, 326 Henry Gould Road, Perkinsville, VT 05151, (802) 263-5410. <vtcanvas@vermontel.net>

Judy Mofield Mallow is a fifth-generation basketmaker and teacher whose work is widely displayed. She runs a basketry supply business, and is author of *Pine Needle Basketry* (Lark Books, 1996). Prim Pines, P.O. Box 148, Carthage, NC 28327. <www.pineneedle.homepage.com>

Linda McNally creates original needlework in the traditional sampler style. Homespun Sampler, 87 Tollgate Road, Warwick, RI 02886, (401) 732-3181. <www.hs-samplar.com>

Cliff Monteith designs and builds rustic furniture. P.O. Box 165, Lake Ann, MI 49650, (616) 275-6560.

Jean Tomaso Moore is a part-time, multi-media artist who has been creating art as long as she can remember. She lives with her husband in the hills of Asheville, North Carolina. <LeaningTowerArt@msn.com>

Ted Nichols hand carves collectibles and toys including Noah's Arks, chess sets, barnyard animals, canes, and Santas. Noah's Ark, 29830 Jackson Road, Salisbury, MD 21804, (410) 546-9522. <www.noahs-ark.com>

J. Mike Patrick is a rancher and sustainable development advocate who handcrafts Western furnishings. New West Furniture, 2811 Big Horn Avenue, Cody, WY 82414, (800) 653-2391. <www.newwest.com>

Debra Paulson is a black ash splint basketmaker and fabric weaver. Paulson Training Programs, 15 North Main Street, Chester, CT 06412. <deb@paulson-training.com>

Michele Petno is a mosaic artist who teaches classes on using tile and glass beads to decorate furniture and found objects. Wits End Mosaic, 5224 West S.R. 46 PMB 134, Sanford, FL 32771, (407) 323-9122.

Judy Bryson Quinn makes baskets using traditional and nontraditional materials and methods in the mountains of Western North Carolina. 45 Sunny Acres Lane, Leicester, NC 28748. (828) 683-4404.

David Robinson designs and builds custom rustic furniture. Natural Edge, 515 Tuxford Court, Trenton, NJ 08638, (609) 737-8996.

Sandra S. Rowland makes quilts by commission in her mountain studio, Good Lookin' Quilts. She teaches and participates in fairs. 77 Harper Road, Murphy, NC 28906, (828) 837-2320.

Michael Saari is a master metalsmith who exhibits his work in the United States and Europe. He also teaches and consults. Michael J. Saari Metal Studio and Workshop, 256 Childs Hill Road, Woodstock, CT 06281, (860) 928-0257. <www.michaelsaari.com>

William D. Sarni creates traditional painted gunning decoys. 10 Powers Lane, Hingham, MA 02043, (781) 749-2315.

Rebekah L. Smith paints, restores, and custom-makes boxes, furniture, tinware, and murals. 678 McKinley Street, Bedford, OH 44146, (440) 232-0940.

Russell Snow designs and creates limited-edition folk art whirligigs and markets them through his business, Vermont Windtoys. 891 Ripley Road, Waterbury Center, VT 05677, (802)-244-8940. <snowvt@together.net>

Daniel Strawser, Jr. is a fourth-generation Pennsylvania German folk artist who creates chip-notch carved items from cigar boxes, fruit crates, and shipping pallets. Strawser's work is collected nationally. <www.strawserart.com>

Alice Strom specializes in hand-painted folk art wood carvings. Spirit of America, Rt. 2 Box 358A, Nevis, MN 56467.

Marie Sugar creates primitive and folk art hooked wool rugs. 10320 Kettledrum Court, Ellicott City, MD 21042, (410) 418-4930 <ssugar@erols.com>

Cynthia W. Taylor, a native of the central Appalachian Mountains, makes Appalachian white oak baskets She is also a well-respected writer and curator in the field. 2605 Cypress Street, Parkersburg, WV 26101, (304) 424-6559.

Terry Taylor lends his creative spirit full-time to Lark Books as a writer and designer. In his spare time, he creates and exhibits art in a variety of media. His designs have been featured in numerous publications.

O. David Vance is a sculptor and painter in the tradition of self-taught artists whose work ranges from carved fishing lures to furniture. He is represented in the Smithsonian's National Gallery of American Art. <Odavidvance@aol.com>

Barbra Viall makes appliquéd rugs, pillows, blankets, and scarfs. Heartisan Studios, 3816 Palmetto Court, Ellicott City, MD 21042, (410) 465-6933. <www.heartisan.com>

Ed Vugteveen is a tinsmith who uses hand tools and old world techniques to do restoration and original work in his family business. The Tinner's Shop, PO Box 314, Allendale, MI 49401. <tinner@altelco.net>

Martha Waterman creates quilts in the tradition of eighteenth and nineteenth century wholecloth. Custom Wholecloth Quilts, 10302 Cedar Wapsi Road, Cedar Falls, IA 50613, (319) 266-5291.

Judd Weisburg creates custom rustic furniture, often gathering driftwood from shorelines. Judd Weisburg Designs, Rt. 42, Box 177, Lexington, NY 12452, (518) 989-6583. <aware@mhonline.net>

Aaron Yakim studied with a fifth-generation Appalachian white oak basketmaker. His baskets are collected internationally. 2605 Cypress Street, Parkersburg, WV 26101, (304) 424-6559

—. *America's Folk Art: Treasures of American Folk Arts and Crafts in Distinguished Museums and Collections.* Edited by Robert L. Polley. New York: G.P. Putnam's Sons, in association with Country Beautiful Foundation, Inc., Waukesha, Wisconsin, 1968.

—. *Americana: Folk and Decorative Art.* New York: Art & Antiques, 1982.

Arnow, Jan. *By Southern Hands: A Celebration of Craft Traditions in the South.* Birmingham, Alabama: Roundtable Press, Oxmoor House, 1987.

—. *Back to Basics: How to Learn and Enjoy Traditional American Skills.* Edited by Norman Mack. Pleasantville, NY: The Reader's Digest Association, 1981.

Bishop, Robert, and Jacqueline M. Atkins. *Folk Art in American Life.* New York: Viking Studio Books, Penguin Books USA Inc., 1995.

Creekmore, Betsey B. *Traditional American Crafts.* New York: Hearthside Press, 1968.

Eaton, Allen. *Handicrafts of New England.* New York: Bonanza Books, 1949.

Eaton, Allen. *Handicrafts of The Southern Highlands.* New York: Russell Sage Foundation, 1937.

Fendelman, Helaine W. *Tramp Art: An Itinerant's Folk Art.* Toronto: Clarke, Irwin and Company Limited, 1975.

—. *Folk Art and American Life.* Edited by Bishop, Robert and Jacqueline M. Atkins, with the assistance of Henry Niemann and Patricia Coblentz. New York: Viking Studio Books in association with the Museum of American Folk Art, 1995.

Hartigan, Lynda Roscoe. *Made with Passion: The Hemphill Folk Art Collection in the National Museum of American Art.* Washington, D.C.: Smithsonian Institution Press, 1990.

Kogan, Lee, and Barbara Cate. *Treasures of Folk Art: Museum of American Folk Art.* Compiled by Abbeville Press. New York: Museum of American Folk Art and Abbeville Press, 1994.

Lavitt, Wendy. *Animals in American Folk Art.* New York: Alfred A. Knopf, Inc., 1990.

Lichten, Francis. *Folk Art of Rural Pennsylvania.* New York: Charles Scribner's Sons, 1946.

Lipman, Jean, and Alice Winchester. *The Flowering of American Folk Art 1776-1876.* New York: The Viking Press, in cooperation with the Whitney Museum of American Art, 1974.

Little, Nina Fletcher. *Little by Little: Six Decades of Collecting American Decorative Arts.* New York: E.P. Dutton, Inc., 1984.

Mack, Daniel. *Making Rustic Furniture.* Asheville, NC: Lark Books, 1992.

Mack, Daniel. *The Rustic Furniture Companion: Traditions, Techniques, and Inspirations.* Asheville, NC: Lark Books, 1996.

Mallow, Judy Mofield. *Pine Needle Basketry: From Forest Floor to Finished Project.* Asheville, NC: Lark Books, 1996.

Schaffner, Cynthia V.A. *Discovering American Folk Art.* New York: Harry N. Abrams, Incorporated, 1991.

—. *Self-Taught Artists of the 20th Century: An American Anthology.* Coordinated by Lee Kogan with curators Elsa Longhauser and Harald Szeemann. San Francisco: Chronicle Books, 1998.

Shaw, Robert. *America's Traditional Crafts: Baskets, Quilts, Woodwork, Decoys, Pottery, and More.* Shelburne, VT: Hugh Lauter Levin Associates, Inc., 1993.

—. *Silhouettes: A Pictorial Archive of Varied Illustrations.* Edited by Carol Belanger Grafton. New York: Dover Publications, Inc, 1979.

—. *Southern Folk Art.* Cynthia Elyce Rubin, editor. Birmingham, AL: Oxmoor House, 1985.

Warren, Elizabeth V., with Sharon L. Eisenstat. *Glorious American Quilts: The Quilt Collection of the Museum of American Folk Art.* New York: Penguin Studio with the Museum of American Folk Art, 1996.

Acknowledgments

Writing *By Hand* gave both myself and Veronika Alice Gunter the delightful opportunity to get to know the work of dozens of traditional craftspeople, folk art collectors, and museum specialists around the country who care deeply about America's artistic heritage. In addition to the artists who designed projects and contributed imagery to this book, we'd like to thank the institutions and the people in them who helped us.

Our appreciation and thanks are due to: Janey Fire, director of photographic services, Museum of American Folk Art, New York; Jennifer Bean, visual resources specialist, Museum of Early Southern Decorative Arts, Winston-Salem, North Carolina; Claudia Jew, manager of photographic services and licensing, The Mariners' Museum, Newport News, Virginia; John and Linda Sholl, Sholl Antiques, Norwood, New York; and Julie Yankowsky, rights and reproductions specialist, Shelburne Museum, Shelburne, Vermont. We're also grateful to Lee and Alice Johnson, and Nancy Alexander and Thad Johnson, for kindly allowing us to photograph their beautiful homes.

Many thanks as well to my friend and colleague Terry Taylor for his unstinting help and delightful wit. Thank you to: our very talented art director, Celia Naranjo, for designing this big, beautiful book; to illustrator Orrin Lundgren; to Evan Bracken for his photography; to Hannes Charen for his help; and to Rain Newcomb and Murphy Townsend for their timely organizational assistance. Most of all, thank you to Lark Assistant Editor Veronika Alice Gunter. Her research, writing skills, enthusiasm for the subject matter, and energetic good humor were integral to realizing the book we envisioned.

In closing, I'd like to dedicate *By Hand* to the memory of my mother, Marjorie Morgan Koman.

Index